Public Speaking Beyond Fear

Also by Stephen Outram…

Books:
Advanced Speaking Concepts
Dealers: Buying, Selling & Making Money
There's No Sex in Golf
Life Before

Blog & Articles:
stephenoutram.com

Public Speaking Beyond Fear

By Stephen Outram
Foreword by Simone Phillips

Disclaimer

This product is designed to provide information and motivation to readers. It is sold with the understanding that the publisher is not engaged to render any type of psychological, legal, or any other kind of professional advice. The content of this product is the sole expression and opinion of its author, and not necessarily that of the publisher. No warranties or guarantees are expressed or implied by the publisher's choice to include any of the content in this product. Neither the publisher nor the author shall be liable for any physical, psychological, emotional, financial, or commercial damages, including, but not limited to, special, incidental, consequential or other damages. Our views and rights are the same: You are responsible for your own choices, actions, and results.

Author: Stephen Outram

Date Published: May 1, 2014

ISBN 978-0-9802927-1-8

Publisher: What Else is Possible?
PO Box 1770, Broadbeach. QLD. Australia

Note: Based upon the 2006 book, *Will Public Speaking be the Death of You?* by Stephen Outram, which been substantially revised, updated, and republished as 'Public Speaking: Beyond Fear.'

© 2014 Stephen Outram. All rights reserved. This material may not be reproduced, displayed, modified or distributed without the express prior written permission of the copyright holder. For permission, contact stephenoutram.com

Stephen Outram

Contents

Foreword *By Simone Phillips*	8
Preface *Reviewed & Updated!*	10
Introduction *The Adventure Begins*	12
You! *Functioning Beyond Normal*	15
Pretence, Camouflage and Automation *The Art of Public Speaking*	18
The Power of Fear *An Energy To Be Used*	23
Uncomfortable *Speaking Without Care*	26
Truth and Lies *Setting You Free*	29
Your Value *Are You Worth Listening To?*	33
Who is Listening? *Blind, Deaf & Dumb*	39
Language Systems *The Process of Translation*	45
The Give & Take Talk *Educate, Provoke & Entertain*	54

Communicating *It's Not All Talk*	58
Public & Common Speaking *Speaking, a Whole Topic*	63
Power of Language *Being In Charge*	68
Scapegoats & Sacrificial Lambs *Surviving the Past*	72
Word Weapons *Use Words Wisely*	79
Family Matters *Childish Decisions*	87
Fight or Flight *Sympathetic Reactions*	93
The Messenger *Don't Shoot Me!*	98
Psychic Possibilities *Is It Really Yours?*	101
Amateurs & Professionals *Emotive, Technical or Holistic*	104
Receiving Applause *An Audience's Gift*	110
Characters of You *Who Are You Being?*	115
Heights Unimagined *Inclusive, Expanding Contribution*	122
About The Author *Biography*	126
Toastmasters *Speaking & Leadership Skills*	128
Related Books *Advanced Speaking Concepts*	130

Foreword

By Simone Phillips

It is with great pleasure that I let my fingers loose on the keyboard to write this foreword to *Public Speaking: Beyond Fear*.

Stephen Outram is a wonderful friend of mine who possesses many attributes that have made this book such a pleasure to read. He is a linguist and computer technician with a background in architecture, who combines all his skills to explore and present ideas about public speaking in a totally new fashion. His patience and thoughtfulness play an integral part in this book. He takes the reader, with great care, by the hand whilst delving into deep concepts, through the meandering of word origins, explanations and interpretations.

The insights into 21st century communication were food for thought for me. He showed me that a lot of us perceive verbal communication, called speech, as the most effective way to communicate with each other. The new slant explored in this book, is that speech is produced, filtered and adapted via machines, and yet we still believe that we are its sole producers. This is just one example of how Stephen adds to concepts that will turn your ideas about public speaking upside down, or

180 degrees if you like.

After reading this book I gained an in-depth and clearer understanding about delivering speeches. As a teacher I communicate concepts and ideas, deliver instructions, present explanations and explore possibilities on a daily basis. Concepts presented by Stephen have made me question how I use language and has made me explore new ways to present and check for understanding.

If you speak at all, be it for work, with family members or present seminars then this book will provide you with key ideas and concepts that can add to your life. It may also empower you to go forth and speak more publicly.

Simone Phillips
Dip. Teach (German /English)
Author of *From Caregiver to Caring* and *Mumble and Jumble—Teacher's Guide*
Contributing Author to *Conscious Parents Conscious Kids*

Stephen Outram

Preface

Reviewed & Updated!

The original book was published in 2006 under the title *Will Public Speaking Be The Death Of You*. This revised edition has been substantially rewritten, including additional new content, title and cover.

After the first edition had sold out, and while writing a new book *Advanced Speaking Concepts*, I reviewed the content and realized that I now had more to offer people who were experiencing difficulty with public speaking.

I noted too, that some of the existing content could be improved by discussing it in a different way and, as some 8 years had passed since publishing, there was much more that I could offer from my own ongoing adventure with public speaking.

For those of you who have read the original, you may enjoy reviewing and also discovering something fresh in this revised edition. And if you are a first time reader, then welcome!

My target is to assist you to move beyond the fear or contraction you may be experiencing with speaking, for you to realize that it can be changed and that you have different choices available to you. Further, there is information and tools that you can apply to your speaking as you explore more of this fascinating subject.

What could be different for you if public speaking ceased being a protection and became an adventure?

Coupled with *Advanced Speaking Concepts*, these two books offer a comprehensive, potent and hopefully enjoyable contribution to *your* adventure with public speaking and performance.

Warm Regards,
Stephen Outram

Introduction

The Adventure Begins

Recently someone asked me, "Are you shy?" To my surprise, the first word out of my mouth was "Yes." After many years of working on my public speaking issues and having progressed to writing books, presenting seminars and giving talks around the world, there was still something to be discovered and cleared up.

It was another breakthrough for me because I realized that I was not shy and this was a lie that I had been telling myself for a very long time. That awareness catapulted me to a level of freedom that I had not had before.

Your quest with public speaking is not a journey with a fixed destination, it's an adventure that will continue to unfold before you as you choose to be more and have more. You may think that if you can just get through this one talk, then that will be it! But no, there is always more. So, relax and stop trying to find the end.

The person who asked me the question is Gary Douglas of Access Consciousness. It is testament to his teachings that a question is one of the most dynamic tools we have available. In this book I will ask you many questions.

We are not born shy or fearful. These behaviors are learnt and something that we accept, without question, as the right thing to do. As we get older we forget what was blindly accepted, but the effect of it remains and influences our lives. The good news is that anything can be changed, when you become aware of it. The value of questions is the clarity that becomes available when you hear them and then choose to take action.

This book is designed to facilitate you to a new level of awareness around what you have previously decided about public speaking. It is from greater awareness that you can choose to create a future that is different from your past.

Questions (and other tools) can provide clarity but they will not create the change you desire. It is your choice that creates. **Choice creates.**

Reading this book can catapult you to greater awareness around public speaking, but it cannot choose and create the freedom you desire. That is for you to do.

> What choices can you make to move beyond fear, beyond limitation and beyond anything you have ever considered possible with public speaking?

In my own life I have chosen many times and created something different with speaking in groups, and more. You can to!

Public Speaking: Beyond Fear is designed to assist you in moving beyond the fear that controls and contracts what you can be when you get up to speak to a group of people, large or small. The change that's required and is possible, will affect not only your public performance, but many other areas of your life.

Are you ready to begin the adventure? Let's go!

You!

Functioning Beyond Normal

There has never been, isn't now and will never-again be anyone like you. You are totally unique, have no competition, are incomparable, invaluable and have talent, ability and capacities unlike any other person. In a world where rarity is judged to be of high-value, you are the *only* you on Planet Earth or anywhere!

Society has determined what is "normal" in just about every area of life. For example, there is a scale that measures normal blood pressure and others for exam results; I live in Australia and hear our politicians refer to "...normal, average Australians."

> "Normative influence refers to a pressure to conform with others because we want to be accepted. Here we try to do what we think others want, so the motive is belonging or self-enhancement"—Martin Skinner, Dept of Psychology, U of Warwick, UK.

To be normal and conform is presented as *very desirable* via our upbringing, our schooling and in the way we are taught to function in society. Being above average is considered a good thing, but to be *on the edge* (of the scale) makes many people uncomfortable and to be different and stand out is definitely risky.

When you accept this viewpoint and try creating yourself similar to everyone else, to not stand out, to not be more brilliant than any other, to fit-in and be normal, then you do not acknowledge the difference you are. You contract you to fit into an acceptable range of existence, but there is a problem.

It is not possible for you to fit in; there is nowhere that you fit. One who is unique cannot be something else.

> How much of your unique capacities, personal brilliance and You have you shut down to try and fit into the accepted range of normal existence?

It is this fitting in, this contraction of you that ensures that there is less of you to create with when you speak.

Imagine an athlete who removes their arms and legs and then attempts to move along the race track; what is memorable, the performance or the struggle? Imagine a brilliant student who shuts-down half their brain before an important exam; what is the result? Imagine a 200 watt light that only gets a small amount of energy; can it shine fully and brilliantly? Imagine a public speaker who is quiet and shy; will they be heard?

When you know that there is more of you than you allow to show up, when you find yourself wallowing in the mire of struggle, when the results you are getting are so much less than you know is possible, when you find that you are barely functioning…then ask yourself, "What alternative choices do I have here, in addition to limiting me?"

Limiting you is a choice that you will always have available, just as functioning from the unlimited, unique and brilliant you is a choice that you always have available.

> What other choices do you have available that you have never chosen?

When you become aware-of and acknowledge your differences, and value them, then you can begin to come out of *normal* and expand. When you value you, so can everyone else. Your public get more from you and you'll probably get payed more too!

The way you speak in groups will change when you function from the uniqueness of you and begin to use it to your advantage.

> What is different about you that you have not acknowledged or valued?

Stephen Outram

Pretence, Camouflage and Automation

The Art of Public Speaking

Public speaking is described in The American Heritage Dictionary as the act, art or process of making effective speeches before an audience. Each of these elements can be used to not-speak as you. They are the pretence, camouflage and automation you use to not show up. When you apply these, unconsciously; without being aware of what you are doing, you will create distrust, conflict and separation from your audience.

Do you speak as an actor, an artist, a machine or as you?

The Actor Speaker

Acting requires talent and ability. A skilled actor pretends to be someone else and works to convince the audience of that. To do that they must suspend disbelief of who and what they normally present to the world and temporarily become the new character—it is known as being *in character*. The stage and film actor Cary Grant was reported saying that he kept on acting Cary Grant until he eventually became him.

Audiences expect actors to not-be themselves; they are willing to suspend their disbelief and they understand how it works, but public speaking is different. Your audience is looking for you!

When you speak in groups as not-you, by acting and playing a character, are you creating a deception? How much of you is actually present and who is really speaking? Can the audience trust what is being said when it's not you saying it?

>   Who are you being if you're not being you?

Many people would rather act than show up as themselves. They prefer to learn lines, do role play or substitute characters rather than appear as they truly are. They have thousands of ready made speeches for any given situation, which are delivered at whoever will listen. You may hear the same speech reused like a worn cardigan. These people have no real interest in you. Walk away and they will immediately find another pair of ears at which to deliver their lines.

Many professional speakers rehearse and learn lines to be able to deliver the same seminar, word-for-word, to every group. It can appear polished and so well presented that you might believe they are really interested in you. Yet they are actors creating pretence and illusion, show after show.

>   Do you speak as an actor or as you?

Acting is not wrong; it can be a terrific tool to use. Acting can be a part of your speech, where your audience knows you are performing a certain segment for them, but if you pretend to be someone else as your speech…they will find you out; they will know and you will lose them.

The Artist Speaker

The artist has speaking down to a fine art. They are experts at interpreting, stylizing, duplicating, replicating, plagiarizing or speaking in the abstract. Can you ever comprehend what they say? Can you ever say what they can comprehend? They speak to create an impression of superiority and use words and phrases in a way that sounds amazing and means little. They know all of the big, obscure words and elucidate them with outrageous flair and panache.

Do you ever know who you are speaking with? Is there ever any real connection they make with their wide-eyed and often bemused listeners? You may have noticed some academics or intellectuals use words that many people would not know, to prove their superiority.

> Have you ever painted pictures with words?

Painting pictures with words is a wonderful skill that can allow your audience to receive what you are saying in a different way. It is one tool, out of many that you have available; do not make it your whole speech.

The Machine Speaker

Machines process language very efficiently and have their own languages. Technology has provided various ways of allowing machines to speak *for* us. E-mail, chat rooms, telephones, text messages, video conferences television, movies, etc; there are myriad ways that machines can represent you.

Is the voice you hear or the vision you see really the speaker? No! It is a digital representation of what was;

a history, an archive. Is the message you hear time and time again on an answer machine, perhaps recorded years ago, anything remotely to do with the speaker now? Can you trust what you hear as a recording that is really the language of machines, machine-systems, recordings of the speaker by machines, facsimiles or copies of people who no longer exist?

> How many machines do you allow to speak for you and as you?

When you have learned your speech by rote and can recite it perfectly, word-for-word, then you are playing a recording that is encoded in your head. You have become an automaton—the machine that represents you.

It is important to recite certain passages, quotes, facts or information correctly, but the speech you deliver as a recorded message will turn you into a battery-powered parrot that will eventually run out of "Squawk!"

The Effective Speaker
Being an effective speaker can make you the effect of what you are saying; in the sense that you must have already decided what effect you want to create, before you speak. And in so doing, you are not willing to allow your audience to be effected in what ever way they choose.

The fact is, that once the words leave your mouth you have absolutely no control over them any more; they are free of you! The person receiving them becomes the new owner, and *they* will choose their effect. So, the effect you create in the world is really chosen by others and therefore you cannot effect someone to do what you want, but you can facilitate them in choosing.

Facilitate means "to render easy." It is your facilitation that can ease the choice your audience makes.

Speaking as You
When you cease acting, painting, reciting, effecting, etc, then you can have more awareness of you and what it is to speak as you. Once you acknowledge the prentice, strip away the camouflage and turn off the machinery you may find you. It is you that can consciously choose to use all the elements we have discussed in this chapter, to your advantage.

This chapter is not saying that these things are bad and don't use them; it's about you not using them, *unconsciously*, as a substitute for you. Acting, art with words, recalling facts accurately, etc, are great tools to enhance your audience's experience and ease their choices. It is you that can facilitate them, not the act of you, not the art of you and not a parrot called you.

The art of public speaking is you, skillfully and consciously applying whatever tools, techniques and methods are required to create the greatest possibilities for you and your audience.

The Power of Fear

An Energy To Be Used

It is widely perceived and promoted that public speaking is the number one fear in the world, even above death. That gives public speaking a certain power to influence. If you will claim the power of public speaking and use it, then you can never be a victim of it, have the fear of it or have it used against you.

How much power is there connected with the number one fear in the world? How much power did Martin Luther King or Adolf Hitler have when they spoke to large groups? They both used public speaking as a tool to influence their audiences. Anthony Robbins, a contemporary inspirational speaker, uses the power of public speaking to educate many thousands of people and receives huge amounts of money, fame and adoration.

> What are you unwilling to receive and claim as yours, of the power of public speaking, that if you did will shift you from victim, to being in control?

Audiences will admire someone who stands up and speaks out. Why? Because often, they are afraid to do it themselves. They may not always agree with what is said, but they respect someone who can do what they can't. They may see a leader.

Those who are willing to stand up and speak out can have power. Are you willing to have that much power?

What changes could you facilitate in the world? Would you be noticed, seen and heard? What could you present to the world as a public speaker? Where would you lead?

The fear of something is a way you distract yourself from having the power of it. It is an invisible cloak that is hiding what's really going on.

> Imagine opening the door to a dark, silent room and refusing to go any further; you can't see what is inside and you are full of fear. You go away but return and open the doorway many times, perhaps over years, or your lifetime. Each time you become a little more curious and begin to reach around the door frame, into the darkness, and search. One day you reach farther than ever before and discover something; a switch. You take a deep breath and throw it.
>
> The room is instantly filled with brilliant light and for a moment, your eyes are blinded. As they become accustomed to the light you look into the room and see a fluffy pussy cat, who walks over and meows at you. You pick her up, stroking the soft fur and feeling the sensation of her purr vibrating in your chest.
>
> All fear is gone and you are calm; peaceful. Now you know what the room is all about and you release the cat at the familiar doorway and turn off the light.

You close the door and walk deep into the darkness, turning to face it.

The power of darkness is yours now and you wait, to set the next person free.

In a similar way this book is a doorway with, I hope, many light switches for you to discover and throw. You may come back many times to open pages, chapters and reach inside further and further. It will be there until every light has been turned on and you are free to choose more of you.

Uncomfortable

Speaking Without Care

When you *care* what other people think about you; about what you say, you cannot say what you would truly like to say. There can never be a freedom or joy in how you speak and what you speak about. You are always in-defence when you care that others will judge you.

During a seminar I gave on public speaking, a participant Dr. Andy Rogger-Amies described to me how he had once given a talk to a group of 20-30 medical colleagues. He was very careful about what he said in case he said or did something stupid. Dr. Rogger-Amies thought that his peers might know more than he did and would judge him harshly for any slipups or indiscretion. This created difficulty for him in delivering the speech because he was watching every word, and speaking from a place of guarded protection.

Speaking in front of a group of professionals can be daunting if you are unwilling to receive their judgements as just interesting. Dr. John Demartini describes how, as a Dr. of Chiropractic, he was asked to give a talk to a convention of dentists. Some of the audience were so irritated and unwilling to be lectured by a chiropractor on dentistry that they got up and began to walk out.

The Master of Ceremonies admonished them and recommended they sit down and give the speaker a chance—not an encouraging beginning for the young chiropractor. Demartini gave his talk, which was so revealing and enlightening to the dentists that he was asked by the audience to continue speaking to them for an additional hour!

> Where have you been unwilling to say what you know for fear of being ridiculed, put-down, unaccepted and rejected by your peers, and those you stand-under?

When you are being careful, guarded or fearful, you are in-defence, the drawbridge is up, the doors are locked and barred, the guns are loaded and you are secured inside a fortress of your own creation. Guess what? You are the only one who has the key. If you are hiding behind stone walls who can see you, who can hear you, who will applaud you, who will appreciate you and who will be grateful for you? No one! No one will know that you are there.

The word fort, as in fortress, is a key part of the word comfortable. When you function from the apparent safety of your com-fort-zone, can you really be present here and now? How many comfort-zones have you created where you hide hoping that someday, someone will hear your muted call, unlock the door and set you free? The reality is that your fortress is made of glass and everyone sees your discomfort, your pain, your frustration, your suffering and wonders why; when the chains that bind you are all unlocked and the doors that bar you are all broken.

Comfort is about you being part of the crowd; a member of the herd. As a speaker you have chosen to be out front and in the spotlight. You will be judged (it's a given) and it's not a comfortable space, but it is where you would like to be or you wouldn't be reading books like this one. It is from the energy of uncomfortable that you can create. Uncomfortable demands much more of you, whereas comfortable makes absolutely no demands.

> What will it take for you to speak without care? What would that look like and what would it take for you to see it as a possibility?

Speaking without care is not about speaking uncaringly. There is a teaching in Toastmasters International that councils, "Know your audience" and a fellow Toastmaster explains it humorously with, "Don't tell pork sausage jokes at a Jewish convention." Access Consciousness teaches its facilitators to, "Talk to what people can hear." Take note dear reader, and do not abuse your audience with your uncaring words.

To speak without care is to receive all judgements and still be you, to be able to receive the viewpoints of others and not be the effect of them and to not have to *do* anything with someone else's stuff.

It can be uncomfortable, but really, that is where you will create from. Being on the edge, the fringe or beyond normal is where everything new and different comes from.

Truth and Lies

Setting You Free

The truth varies from person to person and culture to culture. From a young age we are indoctrinated with moral obligation; an imperative to tell the truth. Lying is judged an offence both at home and in public; liars are often punished and can be jailed. What we learn can have a powerful effect on what we are willing to say or not-say.

My target with this chapter is to invite you to look at how you are functioning on autopilot with instilled viewpoints and beliefs that you have accepted as true. It may seem an odd topic to introduce in a public speaking book, but these can be a major impediment to you having greater ease and freedom with what you're willing to speak about.

You will discover that the truth is different to what is true, and the truth may be a lie that's got you well and truly hooked!

The Truth

The truth is a highly malleable thing, though few will see it as that. The truth is largely considered to be something that never changes and therefore must always hold true, but is it? As a child, I was taught to speak the truth and not to lie, but what is the truth and what creates a lie?

The truth is based on decisions that are often founded upon a belief, or a belief system.

In Christopher Columbus' day people believed the earth was flat and spoke that out as the truth. Was is the truth or was it a lie? The answer is neither; it was simply a point-of-view that was judged to be right and therefore all else must be wrong.

When it was discovered that the earth was round, another point-of-view was created as a new belief that became the truth. Until that new version of the truth was widely circulated amongst the population, the uninformed continued to tell the truth-now-a-lie that the earth was flat; it was the truth for them until something different was presented. They had not actually seen the evidence as Columbus had, so they had to believe he was telling the truth.

Based upon their belief that Columbus was not lying and had told the truth, they created a new point-of-view and the earth became round for them; that then became the truth.

Some people will remain silent unless they can prove what they say is the truth. Others are willing to speak-out what is the truth for them, and try to change the beliefs of those who will listen. If they can get enough people believing what they say, then that may be proof enough for the majority and those beliefs can become widely accepted as the truth.

The truth, is something that people use to justify what they do and how they control others. If I say to you,

"The truth is that the earth is flat and if you go to the edge you will fall off and die!" and you believe me, will that affect how far you are willing to travel?

What other truths are there controlling what you will or won't do or say? For example, If you believe it is the truth that a certain people are likely to attack you, would you be willing to travel to their country and speak at a conference, even if they paid you a lot of money? Probably not!

If your truth is that it is evil to swear, then you can never get paid for being a stand-up comedian in a blue club. If your truth is that Gypsies are thieves, then it will be difficult for you to receive money or goods from them. If it is your truth that being the President is a really dangerous job, then it's unlikely that you'll aspire to that position and make speeches that change a nation.

Your truths and the beliefs they are founded upon are simply points-of-view, often not yours to begin with, that you may have created your whole life upon. What could be different, if you became aware that little of it, if any, was yours?

> What are the truths that are not yours, that if you will simply let them all go, would give you more freedom to be you and speak as you?

You need to know what is true for you, so that you can make conscious choices rather than running on autopilot with no awareness of what is or is not, driving you.

What's true is different to the truth. What is true is

simply what is, and it is that whether you believe it or not. Here are a few examples of what's true: gravity, our bodies require air to breathe, the earth revolves around its axis, concrete is harder than lead.

The Lie

Now, here's the weird twist in the truth/lie story. Do you recall in the Introduction that I described being asked if I was shy? Well, being shy was something that was the truth for me, that I had bought from someone else, that turned out to be a lie I had been telling myself my whole life.

I had built a whole personality on that one lie and created an inability, perhaps a disability around having any ease or fun with public performance.

After Gary Douglas had asked me if I was shy and I had replied, "Yes" he paused and then asked, "…or is that the lie you have been telling yourself?" It was a lie! The moment I acknowledged it, it was gone from my world and has never affected me again.

You need to know what is true for you so that you don't get hung up on the lies. When you discover and acknowledge the lies that seem to be the truth then, much can change for you.

And that…is true!

Your Value

Are You Worth Listening To?

When you try and prove your value; that you are worth listening to, you can create a diminishment of you. We are taught to prove just about everything and various standards are applied to measure our results or performance. What could be different if you spoke beyond that training and beyond the accepted standards?

My Mum recalls how Dad would collect stories throughout his day, so that when he got home in the evening he could always tell her something of interest.

Later in my life, I noticed that Dad preferred to know when I was going to visit him. I realized that this gave him time to gather together some stories so that we wouldn't run out of conversation; there would always be something to fill any gaps. If I dropped-in unexpectedly, then he would be unprepared and that could be uncomfortable. And by the way, I enjoyed my Dad's stories.

He liked to be interesting and informative and he thought that people would value and like him for that. It was sometimes difficult to penetrate the shield of stories that he used, and I'm not sure that I knew my

Dad very well in those days.

It's different now as we are both more willing to create our conversations when we get together. As we are living our own lives and don't see each other as much as we used to, those meetings are so much more expansive and fun when we create them in the moment, rather than planning what they must be.

Where are the places in your life that you are trying to create the value of you? Where do you use your stories, experiences, degrees, papers, qualifications, certificates, licences and tickets to prove that you have value and are worth listening to?

Do you collect bits of information, trivia, read the newspapers everyday to be informed; store away little stories and jokes so you will always have something interesting to say and never be caught-out with nothing to say? How much of you do you trivialize to be interesting? And are you using all of that and more as as a substitute; a replacement for that which is most interesting about you?

From our very early school days we are asked to prove our value, measured by what we do. When doing math assignments, for example, students are asked not only to have the correct answer, but to prove how they got it. It seems that the correct answer is not the correct answer without proof.

When we are older, education can be used to prove that we are worthy of a particular job. A degree or other measure demonstrates a certain level of education considered useful for that job. Work experience in other employment may also contribute to our total value score. All of this objective information can be presented in a résumé. Then an interview, to see if we measure up personally and are not too weird, is added to the list of credentials presented. A positive interview may result in an offer of position.

So, value is first judged objectively and then subjectively at an interview. The greater the perceived value, the greater the salary and then you can be judged by your colleagues and friends based upon how much money you earn. Someone who earns lots of money can be judged successful, which means they have managed to attain a high-value rating…and so it goes on.

> What's your measure? What do you use to score the value of you and how much are you actually worth?

As a speaker, do you have to prove you are worth listening to, or could you simply be worth listening to?

I mentioned earlier on that this book has been substantially reviewed and updated from its first 2006 edition. Previously, the Introduction was dominated by my story; my history of struggle with public speaking. I described my early wretchedness and disability, and how I rose out of the mire to now be presenting my own seminars.

You'll notice, that story does not appear in this book. Why?

That Introduction; my story was me proving to you, dear reader, that I am qualified to write this. I was saying, "Hey. I've been there and done it so I know how you feel." But can I really know how you feel, what you're going through and what you would like to create? No! That introduction is gone now because I do not need to prove me and you do not require me to be proved. You can read this book and choose what will work for you.

My story, as proof, does not provide you with anything that you can use to create change, however, you can use my story to reinforce your own wretchedness and that is not my target. Parts of my story, used as examples of how I created change in the area of public speaking can assist you.

What is valuable is you choosing and creating something different, that works for you.

The truth is that you are invaluable; beyond value. We discussed in the chapter "You!" that you are unique. As a unique person speaking out as you, you will always offer a different point-of-view. When you retell stories (even your own), which are often other people's stories, which they picked up from other people…can you really offer anything new or different?

What is it that you know and what do you have to say that no one else can say like you? Could anyone else have delivered "I Have a Dream" the same as Dr. King? No! Many have tried and they did it the way they did it.

Stop trying to speak out as the proof of you and speak as you? The reality is that this faux value, this proof is always defined by someone else. Whose values are you being measured by? Who is setting the standards by which you must prove you? Are you creating your life based upon a set of standards that limits what is possible for your life.

The lid on a jar of fleas limits how high they can jump. After a while they begin to jump just short of that imposed limit. The fleas have been effectively trained to function within certain limits and continue to do so after the lid is removed.

> How effectively has your training limited what is possible for you?

Will you cease trying to value you, based on some adopted standards. Stop proving that you are worth listening to and give up trivializing you in favour of perfecting the appearance of the interesting, intelligent and informed person that is not really you? Will you speak out as you?

If something is invaluable (that is, beyond value) then valuing it actually creates devaluation. If something is already priceless and you attach a price to it, then it becomes less-than priceless. Where have you been valuing you so as not to be the unique, incomparable, invaluable, priceless and totally magnificent you?

When I was a young boy I learned how to ride a bicycle. I was so excited by this new skill that I pedalled around furiously demonstrating how well I could ride; calling out to my friends, "Hey! Look at me. I know how to ride." Now, 40 years later I know that I know how to ride a bicycle and have no need to prove it to anyone. It is no longer a measure of the value of me; it just is.

Do you have friends who are always trying to prove how good they are? They seek to win every competition, take on every dare and play their favorite game of "one-up-manship" at every opportunity. This game always involves diminishing someone else so that they appear superior. They try to make every situation competitive to continually demonstrate they are better than you or someone else. Are they fun to be with?

They are trying to prove that they are better because they think that they are less. They cannot really be better or worse, they are simply different. We are all different. Have you noticed?

Stop pretending to be someone else; choose you. Stop practicing and trying to improve someone else's speech or performance; create yours. Work to up-skill, craft and enhance you. Invest in you. Add to your life. Expand and grow your capacities. You are the gift that everyone is looking for, that no-one else can be.

Who is Listening?

Blind, Deaf & Dumb

Assuming that your audience is "getting" what you're saying can be a mistake and if you are relying on your audience "listening" to you, to get your message across, then you may have limited success!

Listening can be a barrier to receiving, which people use to filter-out parts of what someone is saying to them. And if you are listening intently to your audience, then you may completely miss their message to you.

Listening, even active listening is not a great way to really *get* what someone is trying to communicate. In fact, if you are listening efficiently then you probably won't get it at all. The way you listen to someone can greatly reduce what you are able to receive from them, and what you cognitively come to understand of what they said. What you end up with is your interpretation of what you thought they said, which as I found out, can be very different to what they thought they said to you. Confused? Well, that's what listening is all about.

A very beautiful and much-adored girl friend of mine is called Joella. We dated for several years and among other things, had many wonderful discussions. Several of these could be called high-level, which is a technical term for *argument*. During these high-level discussions, I came to realize that there were places in our relationship where we were communicating really poorly. We were misinterpreting what the other was saying and that led to chronic misunderstanding, anger, separation and unhappiness.

We talked about this and came to an arrangement that when something was said that pushed some buttons, the one reacting would say "Okay, this is what I'm getting here." They would then go on and describe their interpretation of what they had heard. Often this interpretation was so different to the original intent that it was quite shocking.

Our conversations would have been odd to listen to as I would say something followed by "What did you hear just then?" Joella would provide her version and then we would adjust the phrasing until we both got close to shared comprehension. As you can imagine, this was a laborious process and at times it seemed easier to simply be misunderstood.

Clarity came to me when I became aware of what listening really is and how it affects what we actually hear. Listening is a tool that *we* use to filter sensory information that the body receives; in particular, though not limited to, sound.

Speaking is what the body does

Your body speaks and creates the sounds that come from its mouth. Crying and laughing are forms of speaking. These are communications that require no learning and are easily received by everyone i.e. you *know* what is being expressed when somebody laughs. When we articulate, we direct the body into communicating a specific learned-language such as English or French.

Hearing is what the body does
Your body is willing to hear and receive all sound and auditory information. Are you? Unless there is physical damage or the ears are covered, its ears are always switched on. They are part of the physiology that your body uses to alert it to danger or pleasure and they are always on. How much of what your body *hears* do you receive?

Listening is what You do
Listening is a tool that you use. Listen actually means "to list, to catalogue; a boundary or limit." While the body is hearing all sound available to it, you are listening and meticulously filtering out what you don't want to know about.

I recall being at a lively party one evening and noticed a baby fast asleep in its rocker. The music was blaring out and people were talking, dancing and having a good time. The baby slept-on undisturbed as if it didn't hear a sound. Its body heard everything while the baby was busy listening; it simply filtered out the noise and allowed its body to rest.

> How much of what is available to you, do you unconsciously filter-out so as not to receive it in your life?
>
> What have you determined you will or will not receive based upon the way you listen?

Your filter system is a powerful and efficient tool that you have customized specifically for your use. It is a categorized, indexed and searchable database full of all your beliefs, belief systems, opinions, hopes, dreams and goals; everything you've bought as yours from others—the lies, proof, stories, definitions, history, distractions, judgements, decisions and viewpoints that you use to create boundaries and limit what you will receive.

> Do some deaf people listen so effectively that they receive no sound?

When you filter unconsciously, then you are limiting your choices; you may be unaware that you even have a choice. If you have made a decision, for example, "Work is going to be the death of me." then that is added to your database and you can begin to filter out possibilities around work showing up in your life. You could simply miss a great job by not seeing an advertisement, literally, right under your nose.

> Is the way you listen creating the blindness, deafness and dumbness of you?

The body is a magnificent sensory instrument. It is designed to provide you with information. What would it take for you to be willing to have all of the information the body receives for you?

The two key things here, are to be aware that:

1. Your audience is filtering everything you say and the majority will only receive a small portion. During a seminar, for example, I asked several participants to give a 3 minute talk. When they had finished, I asked various members of the audience to say which words they remembered. The speakers were shocked. Most people could not recall more that 3 to 4

memorable words, let alone a full sentence.

2. You too, are listening to your audience with your ears, eyes and other senses. In addition, you are probably listening to yourself as well; the filter can work both ways.

I mentioned in another chapter that Access Consciousness recommends that you "Speak to what someone can hear…" as an addendum to that I would add, "…and be aware of how someone is listening to you." If you ceased to listen, could you become more aware of what someone, or a group of "someones," can receive?

How would you do that?

Awareness is not so much *a how* and more *a choice*. Asking yourself questions, to gain more awareness, is a good place to start. For example:

- Is this person/s getting what I'm saying?

- What am I missing here?

- Do they have any interest, at all, in receiving what I'm saying?

- How else can I present this [information] to assist them receiving more?

- What other choices do I have here?

When speaking to one person or a group, you can create greater connection and a more successful communication with the audience if you are willing to receive from them.

With Joella, I was speaking and listening at the same time and was unaware of the confusion and misunderstanding I was creating. When she spoke to me, I listened so intently that I didn't hear what she was really saying.

I had been taught that if I listened with focus and paid attention; if I did Active Listening, then I would understand. It doesn't really work. The reality is that had I ceased to listen and been willing to receive more from her, then I would have known what she was saying or getting of what I was saying. There would have been no confusion, no misunderstanding and no separation if we had totally received each other. What else would have been possible for us if we created our relationship from that space, of *totally receiving each other?*

Perhaps your body might teach you a lot about hearing and receiving. It doesn't judge what it hears, it doesn't make one thing good and another bad, it simply receives.

What could be different for you if you came out of listening and started to hear?

Language Systems

The Process of Translation

As a speaker of language; words are one of the more obvious and main tools you have to work with, though not the only tool. It is important to understand this tool and be aware of where it can work against you.

There is a process of "translation" as your words pass from you and onto someone else. The translation and re-translation of an original or source piece of information can modify the original in remarkable and unexpected ways. If you are expecting language to work and convey your ideas accurately, then you may be disappointed.

Language

Steve Biddulph, in his book *Manhood*, notes that young children learn to communicate and speak a language in just a few years with no formal training. In addition, if there is more than one language spoken in the home, then they will learn those as well.

He goes on to say that it is bizarre that it takes another ten or so years to teach them to read and write a single language at school. It seems that speaking is something we can do quite easily, though learning how we speak and formalizing that as words on paper is so much more difficult.

Students these days generally work with greater ease

on a computer or smart phone keyboard than they do with traditional pen and paper. Perhaps it is because they don't have to try and remember the linear-system of 26 characters that make up the English alphabet; it is right there on the keyboard. The word alphabet may be a subtle combination of two words, alpha and habit, meaning first or prime habit. Interesting? What do you know about language?

Language simply means "the tongue," from Latin lingua. It is peculiar that contemporary dictionary definitions lean strongly towards "systems of communication" and "systematic communication," which suggests to me that languages are complex programs that are more suited to machines than people. For example, computer software like *Microsoft Word* is programmed with the rules of grammar and can offer corrections to the typist, instantly, as the document is being created; similarly with spelling.

Typing on a computer is called word processing and the machine can process words much more efficiently than a person, though machines are limited in speaking convincingly.

Translation
With the Internet and smart phones becoming more and more popular and the preferred way to communicate, our language is being digitised. A digital language system is binary—zeros & ones—it is the basis of the language of machines.

When you sit at your computer and type an e-mail, the software is invisibly converting your message into Hyper Text Markup Language (HTML). When you press the send button, the computer re-translates or encodes the HTML into a binary language via something called MIME and then transports it to the destination computer, which translates it again and displays the message ready to be read.

When you make a phone call, a computer translates your voice's audio information into a machine language-system, which is translated again at the receiver's phone. Is it really you speaking or a machine speaking for you?

Within all of that translating, does anything change of what you say and how would you know if it did? If subtle changes were made in-translation, would the person you are speaking with really get what you meant to say? The reality is that they are receiving whatever the machine has provided to them, on your behalf.

What if the translation software was flawed? Could it deliver what you said and if not, would that create confusion, misunderstanding and separation? Be aware that while machines can make communication faster over time and distance, some things may be better said in person.

When you speak with someone face-to-face, is it really you speaking or your body? It's your body! You, the being, sends energy to the body, which translates that and produces it as sound. The body you are speaking to receives that sound and translates it into energy so the being receives it. So, is sound energy? Yes. When your computer sends an e-mail for you, does it send it as electrical energy? Yes. Is there really any difference or is it simply all energy?

If you are willing to receive all information as simply energy, rather than the illusion that it is something else, would you be communicating using the core language, energy? If there was no requirement to translate everything you send and receive, could there ever be any confusion, misunderstanding or separation? Is all translation flawed because the original becomes a copy that is changed in the process; and every copy is different to the original? In the game of Chinese Whispers, is the original message and the final translated copy even remotely similar?

When I was about nine or ten years old we lived in Port Hedland in Western Australia and my Dad took me to join the Scouts. One weekend my scout group went on a camping trip and in the evening, all gathered around a blazing camp fire, we played a game of Chinese Whispers.

There were about 20 boys and the Scout-Master began the game by whispering a short phrase into the ear of the first boy. Over the next 15 minutes or so the message was passed in a whisper, ear by ear, until it reached the last boy.

As the message journeyed further around the circle the boys receiving it laughed and became quite noisy. Finally the whispering stopped and the last Boy Scout was asked to repeat what he had received. His face turned bright red, he refused to stand up and would not speak – we all found it very amusing.

Our Scout-Master took the boy off to one side where the boy whispered what he had heard. We didn't find out the result until the next day because we were all immediately sent off to our tents and bed. Later, the young scout revealed that the message was so rude that he had promised on his scout's honour never to repeat it – a solemn oath for a scout.

Be aware that most, if not all, communication is translated and changed in some way. It becomes virtually impossible to get the original message even if you are standing face-to-face with someone. The original information is created in the moment and changed even before you body hears it. From that moment-on it is a copy that is translated and changed and every time that occurs, its likeness to the original diminishes.

Everything in this world is changing all the time; for what reason would you expect what you say to remain the same? On what basis would you expect everyone to get what you say in the same way? Will you consider the possibility that everyone gets you and what you say differently?

> How much energy do we use continually translating everything sent and received?

The only way to know what is being communicated, is to *know* what is being communicated.

> What do you really know about language and communication that you have not been aware of?

Speaking a Language

Speaking a language, for example the English tongue, requires you to learn that system of communication. That learning, for some, is an ongoing process that can take a lifetime as they study to unravel the mystery of words and their combinations. Speaking a learned linear language-system is a cumbersome and ineffective method of sharing information; it is however the most common.

If another person has learned another language-system such as Japanese, then you won't be able to communicate with them using language. If both people have learnt the same system, it's rare that they will fully and easily comprehend what is said. First, they must analyze the information received by comparing it to their version of English, and then process what they come up with through their listening filter. Can two or more people really receive the same message in the same way? The answer seems to be another question - Are any two people the same?

> Have you misidentified and misapplied learning and speaking the systems of language as true communication and the only choice for communication?

Misunderstandings are common among humans using language to communicate. In fact, misunderstandings seem to be normal whereas comprehension and clarity are less common.

It appears that the use of language can create confusion, misunderstanding and separation and through the many ways it is translated, cause the original information to be changed. Can you trust language to deliver what you intended? Not really; it is however the most widely used and accepted method of communication on the planet. Isn't that interesting?

Is language a limited way to communicate? Language is made up of sub-sets and sub-systems, it is modified to fit language-groups through idioms, derivations, dialects, accents, colloquialisms and other variations. Therefore it is understandable that we misidentify and misinterpret.

> Have you bought the idea that language is the only choice for communication and is it really working for you?

Speakers

As a speaker, you will use language to communicate with your audience; recognise its limitations and be aware of what you create when you use it. If you are willing to be aware of what's happening to your audience as you speak, then you can change what you are saying or doing as they change what they are hearing.

You have more tools available to you than words and language. Your body is an amazing and sensual instrument for gifting and receiving information. Sir Isaac Newton said of the hand,

> "In the absence of any other proof, the thumb alone would convince me of God's existence."

Your body is a magnificent communicator; it might teach you a thing or two if you would let it. Will you?

Watch a mime artist use only their body to communicate; it's an extraordinary and refreshing thing to experience. We keep expecting to hear some words because we are so used to that being the method of communication; but they do not come.

Close your eyes and listen to a singer communicate with music. With your eyes closed you can't see their body, but hear only their voice; their song.

Keep your eyes closed and listen to a single violin talking to you without any words at all.

Sit on a quiet hillside and watch the sun set into the ocean; what is nature communicating to you with that?

Know that language is not your only choice.

> "Words are a pretext. It is the inner bond that draws one person to another, not words."—Rumi

Nature holds nothing back, it gifts you the total abundance that it is without judgement.

A flower communicates to you its beauty without ever saying one word; you get it immediately, fully and without limitation and you are willing to receive that totally.

> "I want to sing like the birds sing, not worrying about who hears or what they think."—Rumi

What is *that* communication and what would it take for you to gift that to your audience? That's you, all of you, fully, abundantly and without limitation.

What sort of communion could you create if you were willing to be, do, have, create and generate without limitation?

What change could you create in the world if you communicated as you?

Stephen Outram

The Give & Take Talk

Educate, Provoke & Entertain

The Give & Take Talk is used by many speakers. You will find it in politics, public forums, formal events and the like. It is a speech designed to deliver information and invites no contribution from the audience, other than to sit there and take it.

The National Press Club (NPC) of Australia regularly hosts speakers, who address professional journalists. Often, the speaker reads from a prepared, written speech and then takes questions. The most interesting part is question time. Not only because the journalists get to ask about what they are most interested in, but because the speaker must ad lib; respond spontaneously and can speak more freely.

The first part, the read speech, is the Give & Take Talk, where the speaker *gives* a speech and the audience *takes it*. The second part, question time, is much more of a conversation where speaker and audience include each other. I have observed speakers being much more at ease, often there is shared humour and a sense of mutual respect.

The barrier of the Give & Take Talk is removed with the invitation and inclusion that questions facilitate. And the journalists get to stand in the spotlight, be heard and contribute in a way they cannot during a read speech. Question time is an example of gifting and receiving, with public speaking.

Truly great public speaking is all about gifting and receiving with your audience, and not the limited viewpoint around only giving. Most speakers get up to *give a speech* and don't consider *receiving the audience* as a possibility with which to create a *real connection*.

Many people approach a conversation with the attitude of *giving their opinion* and don't consider the possibility of *receiving another viewpoint*, which might change their lives. Some people use public speaking as a way of creating separation, which can lead to confusion and distrust. Can there ever be an expanding joyfulness in communication when functioning from that? Are you looking to create a limited, contracted communication with public speaking or will you consider another possibility?

Many events will require you to provide a written, prepared speech and in the main you will be asked to deliver that. Be aware of what you create with the Give & Take Talk and be willing to be different. In 2012 at NPC, author Clive James brought no written speech and spoke spontaneously. He had some quotes and several items from his books and gifted a wonderful 50 minutes that I shall long remember. He educated, provoked and entertained in his unique and memorable way.

I hope that the story below also assists to provide you with a further example of gifting and receiving. The evening I describe took place many years ago and is still fondly remembered.

>What will it take for your speeches and performance to be memorable for decades?

Sometime in the late 1980s I was delighted to go to one of Sammy Davis Junior's concerts on the Gold Coast, Australia. It may have been the last time he toured Australia as he died a few years later. It was called the *Mr. Bo Jangles Tour* and Sammy was just fabulous!

He came on-stage dressed in a gorgeous tux and had enormous diamond rings on every finger—it wasn't only his eyes that were sparkling—as he walked to centre stage, happily receiving a warm Gold Coast welcome.

When the applause died down, Sammy sat on a stool near a polished grand piano and casually lit up a cigarette. He talked to us with such ease and kidded about smoking and trying to give up cigarettes. Then, one by one he took off all of his diamond rings and put them down on the piano top—thousands of dollars worth of jewelry. He looked at the audience and said, "I don't need all this stuff to be with you guys, it just gets in the way." With that and a brilliant smile, he stepped up and began his first song.

We all got Sammy that night. He gifted us his outstanding talents and abilities, didn't hold anything back and he was willing to receive us totally. He had no need to prove his value and he knew he was unique. He didn't filter us out, received us all and created a unique and glorious connection with the audience.

When he stood silhouetted against the lights after gifting us his finalè song, *Mr. Bo Jangles*, there would have been few in the theatre who were unaware they were appreciated by the remarkable person, Sammy Davis Jnr. He created an intensity of joy that I can recall instantly many years later. Thank you Mr. Davis, for being all of you, for all of us.

Communicating

It's Not All Talk

What does communicating mean to you? When I ask that question, the most common answer I get is, "Talking." Many people have the view that if they are talking then they are communicating. Is that really true or is it just one side of the conversation?

Both conversation and communication are prefixed with co, which means "together and more than one." Communication or its core commune means "to make common, share, general, shared by all or many." If some information, an event or experience is shared by all or many, it becomes common and everyone present has access to it. When you create a common experience for your audience, then it can catalyze better communication. It is quite a thrill when you hear, "Ahh..." rippling across the group you're talking with, as a new awareness is grasped.

Some people will talk *at* you, which creates a one-sided conversation. When someone is talking at you, are they really interested in communication or just pushing their energy at you?

As a speaker, you can fall into the trap of talking *at* your audience, rather than facilitating a shared common experience. Reading a speech is one way of doing that, which is discussed in detail in the chapter "The Give & Take Talk."

You have many choices, in addition to talking, with which to create communication; consider the following:

It is widely recognized that adults like to learn by participating, role-play reinforces theory, children enjoy learning especially when it is presented as games, we all seem to like stories, pictures are instantly recognized and understood, movies are really powerful and effective, appropriate jokes are greatly enjoyed, humour can open doors, questions allow interaction, gifts and rewards are appreciated, objects and examples can provide clarity, variety encourages people to be present, mime artists entertain without speaking, and also there is talking.

Have you bought into the idea that talking is the preferred and only choice for communicating on this planet? Are you really communicating when you talk and does anyone fully comprehend what you say, including you?

Many people will listen to your words and begin translating them into pictures. As you read the words "home" or "car keys," you will probably visualize those objects in your head. While reading a book, you will often create pictures based on the descriptions you see in text and if the sentences are rich with seductive descriptors, the illusion can appear very real.

You receive words, vision and other sensory information converting these into pictures, thoughts, feelings and emotions; which are then interpreted in order to understand what you think you have received; you then take that understanding, create your response, convert it into pictures and then translate it back as words and speak it out in reply. Does that seem like a cumbersome system?

When you are speaking, your audience may be unconsciously creating pictures. When the pictures blur into movies and that becomes more interesting than the words you are delivering, they will daydream. They are gone and you have, literally, lost them.

Words used effectively can be extraordinarily powerful. Words have been used, for example, to change the course of history, to begin or end a life and to start a war. The right words at the right time can change your life. Martin Luther King, Adolf Hitler and other public speakers used words to create massive change in the world.

You will have heard the saying, "A picture is worth a thousand words." So how powerful is one picture and how powerful are ten pictures or a movie made up of millions of moving pictures? Pictures that move fast enough can merge together and appear as a whole new reality; it seems a bit like life.

> The idea that a person must "suspend their disbelief" to watch a movie is attributed to Samuel Taylor Coleridge, 1817 "...my endeavours should be directed to persons and characters supernatural, or at least romantic, yet so as to transfer from our inward nature a human interest and a semblance of truth sufficient to procure for these shadows of imagination that willing suspension of disbelief

for the moment."—Sourced from Wikipedia.

What does this all mean for a speaker?
Well, if you rely on words alone, then your ability to communicate will be limited. I have read information that suggests words alone will only reach about 10% of an audience. Considering all of the translation, interpretation and conversion that your audience will be doing to try and understand what you are saying, the possibility of total communication and comprehension is unlikely. Depending upon your style of presentation you might connect with only about 20-30% of your audience. People will only get what they can get, in that moment. I have attended a seminar and later, listened to the recording five or six times. To my astonishment, on the sixth time, I heard new information that I could swear wasn't there before; and it certainly couldn't have been spoken in the seminar; could it?

Often, the information you are presenting becomes available to your audience some time after your talk; and sometimes not at all. I have often had something leap into my head with clarity and distinction months after attending a seminar. It came when I was willing to receive it, not when the speaker wanted me to receive it. If you speak from a place of facilitating change for people, then you will not get caught in the expectation of when it must happen so that you can measure your success and prove your value.

How you connect with the audience will have a lot to do with your talents, abilities and personal brilliance. What they get out of it and when, is the audience's choice. Don't judge you as being a poor communicator when you don't seem to be getting through. Ask questions and be willing to change in mid-flight. Ask yourself, for example:

- What does this audience require of me?
- What can I do differently to create a greater connection?
- What will it take to expand the possibilities here?
- What's right about this that I'm not getting?
- ...and one of my favorites, What else is possible?

Delivering a fixed, parrot-like, rehearsed performance will not allow you the flexibility to change in the moment and make a difference in what's occurring. As a member of the band, *Blues Down Under*, playing local pubs in south west England, we rehearsed to have a repertoire of 60-70 songs. We only required about 40 songs for a gig but we knew that every audience would be different. If we found they weren't getting into what we were playing, we simply changed the songs until we made a connection. It was much easier and fun after that.

Be aware, follow the energy of what is occurring for your audience and receive what they are communicating to you. And remember, their communication will probably not be talking!

Public & Common Speaking

Speaking, a Whole Topic

When you realize that public speaking is just one part of a larger topic, you can have more choice in the tools and techniques you use when you speak. It makes no sense that public speaking is the only way to speak to groups of people, yet for some it is their only choice.

Public Speaking

Public speaking is used by politicians, lawyers, public servants and others as their preferred method of talking at the public. They have perfected the technique of not answering a question and being able to speak around a topic without actually speaking on-topic. When listening to your country's leaders on the news or being interviewed on television, do you really trust what they say?

Public speaking is a great skill that can be very useful for a speaker in certain forums such as politics, for example, where you may not want to say an outright, "No!" to something, and at the same time do not want to commit to it. It can be fun to observe the interplay; the tussle between journalists, interviewers and politicians. A great example of this is the famed 1977 interview that David Frost conducted with

USA President Richard Nixon. Deceptively easy-going at first, Frost eventually worked an apology to the American public out of Nixon for his role in the Watergate scandal.

Some public figures have the view that if they told the truth, they may be attacked and thrown from office. They speak to defend their position or attack their opposition and function from a constant state of fight or flight.

As I write this chapter, Ukrainian protestors have fought police and armed forces in the capital Kiev to eventually succeed in throwing out elected President Viktor Yanukovych. At the height of the fighting Yanukovych fled and it was reported that no one knew of his whereabouts. The media have labeled this event the "Ukraine Crisis." When public speaking fails, then flight may be a wise choice.

Have you noticed how quickly Presidents and Prime Ministers can age? Within a few short years in office, their hair is greying and they are looking worn out and tired. It is a very hard job and takes a lot of energy to remain in a constant state of war—defence, attack and being attacked. Public speaking can be a tool for staying alive; for surviving.

Common Speaking

Common speaking is a more open and inclusive way of communicating. Common simply means "universal, widespread" suggesting that speaking can include and reach more people.

Common speaking is what you do when you meet with

your best friend for coffee and talk. It is what you do when you are laying in the arms of your lover on Sunday morning after having sex and sharing the moment. It is what you do when your 16 year old daughter confesses to you she is pregnant and you gather her up in your arms and tell her it will be all right; you are there for her. Common speaking is when you truly connect with someone from a place of no-judgement and can say anything, because nothing matters and everything is possible. There is no confusion, no misunderstanding and no separation. There is clarity and communion.

By expanding the energy you are when you speak to a friend, to include more people, a larger group or audience, something different is possible. Make your purpose; your target in speaking large enough to include everyone.

Nelson Mandella for example, who served as President of South Africa 1994-1999, was known widely to the people as "the father of the nation." Many even called him "Tata", a Xhosa word for father. Mandella's target was to dismantle apartheid and free people from its shackles. It was a large target and millions of black South Africans moved to the cities and improved their living standards and education.

> "For to be free is not merely to cast off one's chains, but to live in a way that respects and enhances the freedom of others."—Nelson Mandella

Laughter is received simply and easily, as energy. People who hear laughter often begin to laugh as well. Do you remember those laughing bags that were popular in the 1980s? They were a little machine in a bag that mimicked laughing. The laughter from the bag went on-and-on and in a remarkably short time everyone who could hear it was laughing too—it was totally inclusive and so much fun.

Everyone instantly knows what laughter is. There are no words and no pictures and absolute clarity. Laughter is common and shared by all or many. Likewise, a smile is known world-wide as a greeting or an expression of pleasure, fun, joy and delight. Laughing, crying, screaming, mewing, singing, hugging, kissing, smiling, etc. are all things that you know energetically and they require no translation.

Science tells us that everything is energy. It is common, universal and shared by the many. Is it possible that you could have omni-lingual energetic languages and comprehension as your reality? Is it possible that you could simply know what everyone was saying to you energetically and not have to translate and interpret?

> "The first and greatest language is actually energy."—Gary Douglas

Have you walked into a room of people and been aware of some tension or anger? "I could have cut the atmosphere with a knife it was so thick." What is that? What did you perceive when you walked into that room, energy? Did you require any words or explanation about that or did you instantly know? Have you thought to phone a friend and then the phone rings and it is them phoning you. What did you know? Have you walked down the street and accidentally bumped into someone you know, to discover they really wanted to see you? What did you know? Will you consider the possibility that you were perceiving and receiving the universal lingo, the language of energy?

Many people have the idea that public speaking is the only way to speak to groups, but there is more to choose than that. Speaking is a "whole" topic and includes much more than one or two things.

Both public and common speaking are useful. It is important to understand what they are and be aware of what you create when you use them.

It may seem that common speaking is a nicer "feel good" tool, but there may be times when public speaking might save your life.

You need to be aware of all of speaking and choose what is appropriate, and what will work for both you and your audiences.

> What, of other people's viewpoints, have you bought into that limits your current perception of speaking?

Stephen Outram

Power of Language

Being In Charge

Language is one of the tools that you have available and used well, it has the power to greatly influence audiences. Have you heard someone say, "Wow! He has great command of the language"? When you are willing to be in-command and in-charge of your audience, then you can have their attention.

Despite being a hyperactive and an often out-of-control boy, I recall that my Dad rarely spanked me. There were a few occasions when I had done something extremely foolish, like lighting fires under our timber house, that he used his hand to light another type of fire on my backside; one I can still smell the smoke from. Whew! Dad often used the power of language to control me and when he spoke, in that certain way, I knew to take notice. Mum too, knew of the power of language and used that first to try and regain control when my sister Karen and I were functioning from a state of *high excitement.*

The author of a book, it seems by remote control, can affect you and control your thoughts, feelings and emotions with words and language. They are willing to influence their readers.

Audiences will listen to speakers who are in-command. They are willing to allow the speaker, in varying degrees, to take charge. If the speaker is not willing to be in-charge, an audience can get out-of-their-charge. When an audience is out-of-your-charge, then they become bored, restless and easily distracted.

Imagine you as a powerful electric light bulb attracting moths. Those moths just love the light and come back over and over again; they never get bored with that energy. Turn down the intensity and you get less moths; turn off the light and they are gone.

> Is the way you communicate energized? And what will it take for you to turn-up your pulling power?

A few years ago I read the *Conversations with God* books by author and speaker Neale Donald Walsh. Later, a friend loaned me a video featuring Walsh who was speaking to an audience of several thousand people, which I watched with interest.

He was introduced and came on-stage to huge applause wearing white flowing clothes; his white beard and hair framed a handsome smiling face. It was a stylish entrance. Walsh came to rest centre-stage and looked out to the audience. As he gazed high and low, left and right, it appeared he was trying to look into the eyes of everyone there. He didn't say a word for about a minute or so and just looked at the audience. The silence in the auditorium was immense as Walsh connected with us.

He was so bright in the spotlight and the energy he was creating, grew and grew. Finally, when it seemed almost unbearable, he opened his mouth and softly said, "Ladies and gentlemen, God needs you." That sentence, delivered at that moment was so intense and powerful that we all gasped with the enormity of the concept it presented.

Walsh was silent again for a while, then repeated the sentence and continued his talk. He was in charge, commanded attention and his talk was well received. Silence is a remarkable feature of the power of language. Often what you don't say, is so much more than what you can say. In a world where people try to fill every space with sound, silence can be the difference that will allow you to communicate.

> How much noise do you have filling your silent spaces?

> Where do you dissipate the power of silence with the noise of your chatter?

People making up an audience hope that the speaker will move them, touch them or affect them in some way—that's why they show up, to receive something they think they can't get or don't have. People go to the movies or to a show to be entertained, because they can't entertain themselves in that way and so they seek it elsewhere. Many audiences will actually pay, in the hope that something may change for them; later they might describe it, for example, "I was moved to tears." "She really got to me." "Oh my God! That part, when he said…" It's their measure of how the speaker was able to influence them and it is valued.

Before each talk you do, ask yourself, "What does this audience require of me?" and wait; take a moment to receive the awareness (be it cognitive or energetic) that the question may facilitate. Questions like this can assist you to come out of the view of, "What do I require of this audience?" and begin to create a difference in the way you present and communicate.

You can begin to be aware of your audience and connect with them at the place they are functioning from and perhaps introduce something into your talk that you had not considered before.

In this way, the audience's requirements and your awareness of them, contributes to your talk. And later, perhaps you may hear someone say, "Oh my God! It was like he was talking directly to me. He said just what I needed to hear." And that dear reader is a remarkable gift, when you can facilitate one person in an audience of 100 or 1000 with exactly what they required.

Language is not just words and grammar, it includes many things. What you say, what you don't say and how you say it can influence your audience; the energy you be when you speak and your ability to change in the moment may bring you rewards you could not have imagined.

Stephen Outram

Scapegoats & Sacrificial Lambs

Surviving the Past

This is an unusual chapter, though an important one to explore. The idea is that if you have made decisions about public speaking, that it is bad or life threatening for example, then those decisions can influence how you are with speaking and public appearance. If your decisions were made a long time ago, and you don't remember making them, then you will have no idea why you react the way you do. The good news is that decisions can be undone, when you become aware of them, but while they exist they can be very powerful and binding. And if you are willing to consider it, perhaps some of those decisions were made in other lifetimes when you were someone in the spotlight; a public figure.

Whether past-lives are real for you or you believe otherwise doesn't really matter; it's simply interesting. Is it possible that somewhere in your "existence" you have made a decision or two about speaking to groups based upon what has happened to you, as your experience? You couldn't have a fear of public speaking without some judgments of it, leading to a decision.

Many people create their lives based upon their past experience; their history, which can include past-lives. As a multi-dimensional being those historical reference points used for creation may extend through all time, space, dimensions and realities. If you had created a limiting belief in another lifetime and are looking for the answer in only this one, could you ever get free?

Energy is everywhere; it is the stuff of which everything is made. Would energy be limited to just this reality? If the energy of what locks you up exists outside of your current frame of reference or awareness, then you will be totally unaware of it? You are however, living the results of it and are currently experiencing the effects of it.

The results of what you are experiencing are simply the visible or experiential symptoms of a cause. They are information or clues pointing, sometimes obscurely, to that cause. If you can get to the cause, and change it, then the symptoms will change too, or cease to exist. The key here is to gain awareness of what you're currently unaware of.

A story is told in the documentary film *What the Bleep*, of Columbus' ships approaching the Americas. As the ships sailed-in, closer to the shore, the natives couldn't see them even though the ships were within normal vision range. The local people had nothing in their experience with which to reference these strange objects and simply could not see them.

The tribal shaman noticed the wake that the ships were making as they sailed along the coastline and perceived that as an anomaly. He watched the moving wake for days and finally his brain decoded this peculiar new data and he was able to see the ships. That which had been beyond his awareness, he became conscious of. His expanded awareness made it easier for everyone in the tribe to also see the strange new craft and a new possibility was available to those people.

> What is it that you are unaware of, that if you became aware of it, will set you free?

> What is it that creates the fear and disease of public speaking as real for you?

The Death of You

Now, let me ask you some of the weird questions:

- In how many lifetimes have you been jailed or sacrificed to be killed while speaking out in the name of some just cause, an injustice, representing an apparent honorable person or standing-up for a weaker one?

- In how many life times have you championed someone else's cause and been deserted to stand alone and face the barbs, the stings and the arrows?

- How many times have you thrown your body in front of another and taken the sword for them, the arrow or the bullet?

- How long have you been protecting you from being ripped apart by the crowd, being the scapegoat, having your tongue cut out, being in the firing line, stoned, beheaded, garrotted, hung drawn and quartered, jailed, burned at the stake, gutted, speared, slashed, cut, shot, maimed, nailed to the cross and offered at the altar as the sacrificial lamb?

- How many times have words failed you to protect you?

What do these question bring up for you and how is your body reacting right now? If you are feeling uncomfortable, then you may be beginning to access information beyond your current awareness. This could indicate past decisions, vows, swearings and the like that are still in existence; still affecting you.

Surviving

I mentioned in another chapter that politicians use public speaking for their survival. What about you? Is public speaking a way to defend against being ripped apart by the crowd? And if you perceived you didn't have a high level of skill in the public arena would that create a fear for you? Without the tools, what defense can you raise?

The majority of people when they walk through a dark creepy alley are wary, careful and easily startled. Walking across a deserted park late at night can appear daunting and may cause the sympathetic nervous system to activate, triggering fight or flight. When you are fearful of speaking in groups and get up to speak, you can activate the body's sympathetic nervous system and begin to function from being attacked, setup defenses or become *frozen in the spotlight*. When you stand up to speak and everybody's eyes turn to look at you, it can seem that they have all just taken aim, directly at you!

A house I lived in featured a very beautiful garden. A large stone bird-bath attracted all kinds of birds and it was such a joy to see them drinking or splashing around in the water. Many times when I was sitting quietly on the lawn enjoying the sunshine, the birds walked close-by as they searched for food. While they were aware of me they seemed quite relaxed until I looked directly at them. Then, they become very conscious of me; I had focused the sights and they knew they were in the cross-hairs, and if I moved just then they would take flight. When all eyes are focused on you, you may be screaming to your body, "Run!"

> You can't run because that would make you look foolish and you'd rather be shot than look stupid. So you stay and begin to put up your defenses: you act and pretend that you're just fine, you laugh about an octave higher than normal to release the tension in your jaw, then you have to clamp your teeth together to stop them chattering.

> You put your hands in your pockets to hide the trembling, you speak quickly to disguise your shaking voice, you pace to stop your knees from knocking together and you know if you don't breathe soon it will all be over. You shrink your body size to be less of a target, you squeeze your buttocks together to prevent any accidents, you try to stop your beating heart from leaping out of your chest, you attempt in vain to push your stomach back down to where it should be.

> You contract your energy to be less visible, you wish your head would stop pounding, you lick your lips which have become very dry, you clear your throat which seems full of cement dust, your eyes begin to sting as the sweat off your brow runs in torrents, you

wish you were dead as you open your mouth to say the first word and nothing happens.

You know you look like a fish out of water and now you are suffering dementia and have forgotten your opening lines, you force out some words and rush through your speech, you put your head down and run off-stage, your ears have stopped working and you miss the applause, you hide in the bathroom and try to figure out how you can slip out without being noticed. You swear never to come back and do this again. How does it get any better than this?

Please forgive my attempt at humor, though you may recognize some symptoms and these can be the very real effects of the fear of public speaking. Some studies cite public speaking as the number one fear in the world, even above death and dying. If that is true, then it is a greater problem than is currently being acknowledged. Can you perceive the energy that is locked up worldwide in this fear and the limitation people are living with? What else would be possible for everyone if the fear of public speaking was utterly destroyed and what will that take? What could people say to each other if they stopped functioning from defense/attack and were able to communicate easily?

I'll leave you here with some questions that you may like to ask yourself. Questions have the wonderful ability of opening you up to other possibilities. For example, rather than stating, "Public speaking scares me." ask yourself, "What will it take for me to be free of the fear of public speaking?"

Here are several questions for you to explore:

- What is it that you are unwilling to speak and what is unspeakable for you that if you spoke it, would set you free?
- What are you whispering that you're unwilling to say that if you will shout it out loud, would change your life?
- What words are you avoiding speaking by the words you are choosing to speak?
- What are you saying that no one else can hear?
- What would you like to say that you're unwilling to say, that if you will say it, will allow you to be heard.
- How does it get any better than this?

Word Weapons

Use Words Wisely

There are many stories, quotes, texts and other examples of how words can be used to inspire, motivate and encourage; the area that is not covered as thoroughly is words being used as weapons.

Some of the techniques used to diminish others, such as banter and sarcasm, have become part of the way we interact with each other and are socially accepted, or in some cases expected.

My editor commented that after reading this chapter she felt a little down and was looking for the "positive" side of words. With that feedback, I knew the chapter was working.

When you use words as weapons, to diminish or put-down, know what you create; and be aware of what your target is receiving from you. Words are powerful, both to negate or inspire; neither is bad and both have effect. Use your tools wisely

Words at Work
The broadcasting industry uses words as the key component in radio. Their advertising allows radio stations to make a profit and exist as a business. The illusion is that radio provides free entertainment; the truth is that radio is in the business of advertising. Its

prime purpose is to sell advertising and everything else it does, supports that purpose. All of the shows, your favorite DJ, talk-back, phone-ins, drive-time, news updates and the many quizzes and competitions are all designed to keep you listening so that you will hear the advertisements. Radio stations can provide compelling statistics to prove their value to businesses considering advertising with them—just ask for their media pack.

Magazines use words and imagery for the same purpose as radio; they too are in the business of advertising as is television, newspapers and other media. The longer these businesses can hold you as listening, reading or viewing, then the greater the effect their advertising can have on you. Words are extraordinarily powerful.

Words (including silence) can be used to defend, attack or control. I once dated a girl who, when upset with me, would refuse to speak. I would then try to get her to talk with me to find out what I had done to upset her and what I could do to heal it. Who do you think was in control? Was I judging me as being in the wrong? She used silence to effectively manipulate me, get my total attention and have me in the wrong.

> What strategies do you use to have an affect on others?

Criticism

When someone criticizes you, do you counter attack with some effective words that remind them of their own inadequacies, or do you surrender or withdraw? Perhaps you attack and then they attack until someone looses.

> "Comedian Dan Nainan was arrested after he punched reporter Josh Rogin… who wrote a pair of critical tweets about Nainan's act, which seem to have sparked the altercation."—Fran Berkman of Mashable

Criticize means to "pass judgment, usually unfavorable." It is quite different to feedback, which can be given without a point of view and be designed simply, to provide information. The energy of judgment is distinct and can be delivered effectively with words i.e. the same sentence can be delivered with judgment or without it, and create a completely different effect.

Criticism seems to work well in comedy, politics and of course, critics of the arts and other creative endeavors.

> "A 2012 study by Amy Bree Becker, Assistant Professor at Towson University, found that attitudes about a candidate were affected by viewing critical comedy content, irrespective of whether the viewer self-identified as a Republican or Democrat."—Science Daily

Sarcasm

Sarcasm is described as "a bitter cutting jest" and has been called the lowest form of humor. It is a technique of using words disguised as humor to diminish someone. Often the deception is delivered so skilfully that the victim is oblivious that they have been attacked; they will laugh at the apparent humor to the delight of their smiling assailant.

> "I may be drunk, Miss, but in the morning I will be sober and you will still be ugly."—Sir Winston Churchill

Being sarcastic has the energy of sharp, pointed and cutting; it is the knife's edge or the rapiers point. Be totally aware of the consequences of your choices when you use it, and be very aware when it is being used against you.

Banter

Banter is described as "to attack with jocularity." When I was in my twenties I had a great bunch of mates who all hung-out together, particularly at a pub called the Pacific Hotel located in Southport. It was the oldest pub on the Gold Coast boasting some 100 years. In the late eighties it was knocked down and replaced by a huge shopping complex called Australia Fair.

We were such a good looking lot (yeah right) that sometimes girls would join us for a drink. Game on! It was quite remarkable how quickly the conversation changed once a girl showed up; the swearing ceased, manners appeared and a chair was quickly found for the nice round bottom attached to the lovely girl. We so liked girls; nearly as much as beer.

Once the lovely girl was seated, had a cold drink and we found out her name, the game of banter began; no guesses as to who was the prize. It all started innocently enough:

"Hey Stephen, remember that time you totalled your car because you were so drunk? Ha-ha! And the girl you had with you at the time, did she ever speak to you after that? Ha-ha."

My reply, "Yeah, but that's nothing compared to that junk-heap of a car you're driving now. There is no girl on the planet stupid enough to drive home with you in that thing. Ha-ha."

In our group, the master of the game was a plumber named Tom King and *crikey*[1] he was good. He would quickly get the better of the other players with his quick wit and remarkable knowledge of all our most embarrassing indiscretions. Through a beer induced haze it seemed like the lovely girl, now looking even lovelier, was enjoying the battle and we all figured it must be a great night.

The thing was, once we had all killed each other off, she left. For what reason would she choose from such a bunch of losers? She now knew all of the places where we were idiots and none of the places we were magnificent. Not one of us had been able to ask her who she was, what she liked and would she like to go out for dinner. We were all so busy attacking, defending and playing the game of banter that we couldn't create a connection that may have lead to something more expansive. We generally woke up the next morning, in bed with a headache rather than the lovely girl.

> In how many ways do you use banter and other weaponry to sabotage you?

---

[1] "Crikey," is in tribute to Steve Irwin; an extraordinary Australian who, was passionate about the environment, always spoke out as Steve and connected with people all over the world. He died in 2006 as I was writing the original book.

Sometime in the 1980s I went to see a show featuring the singer Lovelace Watkins. During his performance a table of rowdy lads got noisy. Lovelace stopped singing, silenced his band and called out to them. He pointed them out and said, "Hey! You! Where do you come from?" The rest of the audience all turned to look at their table, waiting for a reply. One of the party yelled out, "Sydney." Lovelace responded with, "From Sydney hey? Jeeez, it must be bloody quiet in Sydney town tonight!" The crowd roared with laughter and the embarrassed revelers quietened down as Lovelace got back to work.

Use banter to your advantage.

In Writing

Words and their combinations are so powerful that they are used to defend whole countries and millions of people in the form of promises, negotiations, treaties and agreements.

Peace treaties have been used for hundreds of years to bind countries into agreeing not to make war on the other. The European Union (EU) is based upon an agreement made up of words that allows the majority of countries in Europe to trade in a free market. A new currency, the Euro, was specifically created to facilitate that. The United States of America negotiated and signed off on a Free Trade Agreement with Australia, allowing the possibility of greater commerce between the two countries. Australia and New Zealand have agreements in place (ANZAC) that are designed to ensure mutual support in the event of one being attacked.

What is the point?
For the majority of people, words and language are one of the first weapons they reach for.

Do you use your tongue as a weapon; your sword of delivery? It is no coincidence that "word" is contained in *sword*. "Language is a two edged sword." Have you received a tongue-lashing or tongue-whipping that ripped you open like a ripe plum? Have you cut someone to the quick with your dripping sarcasm? Have you been cut by words that were so sharp, you didn't realize you were wounded until you saw the blood? Words are extraordinarily powerful.

I hope that this brief review of words as weapons will provoke you to take a critical look at how you use them and the effect you're having, not only on others but yourself.

While you are busy bantering, who gets the prize of you? No one. While you are busy slashing and cutting with your own unique brand of sarcasm, who could ever get close to you and what could you receive? Little. While you are busy creating agreements and strategies ensuring the defense of you, what could ever get past those defenses and see you, hear you or receive you? Nothing.

Stephen Outram

As a speaker, words are one of your main tools; choose them wisely. There may be occasion where you will defend and others where you will attack, be aware of the consequences of your choices and what you create. Once words are released it is very difficult to retrieve them. They are like captured wild birds, now flown.

Family Matters

Childish Decisions

The influences of family are many and varied; some are more obvious and well known than others. Decisions that you made as a child, which worked for you then, may be working against you now. This chapter can not cover all of the circumstances of childhood, but may go some way to encouraging you to question what you created then that can be changed now.

Family and childhood is a big topic, perhaps a book or several books worth all on its own. My target here is simply to bring you to the awareness that not everything that you were taught, bought into or decided was right still applies now. Have you changed? Has the world changed? Is it time to review some of those past reference points?

While overseas and working in West Sussex, England in the late eighties, I made friends with a great couple, Darren and Marguerite Shaw. They had two young boys, Michael and Mark and it wasn't long before I became known as Uncle Stephen.

One evening, the Shaw family had dropped around and we were enjoying a glass of wine and some good company around the fire. The youngest boy, Mark, had a new toy, which he was showing to everyone. It was a doll where all the body parts were attached together with Velcro strips; so that it could be dismantled and stuck back together like a 3D jigsaw. He hadn't yet figured out that it came apart and was just enjoying playing with it whole.

When he came over to show me the new toy, I grabbed the body and then ripped-off the head right before his eyes; it seemed like a fun thing to do. Whoops! Mark was horrified, let out a shriek of terror and the toddler ran from the room as fast as his little legs would allow. All conversation in the room stopped as everyone looked to see what was occurring. There I was with the evidence in hand and a guilty look on my face. "Oh my God! What have I done?"

Quickly, I refastened the doll's head back onto its body and Marguerite and I ran out after Mark to show him that all was well, "Dolly better now." It took some convincing before Mark would even touch it again and I felt bad for ages. I wondered what effect that would have on the young boy as he grew up.

Dr Grey, author of the book *Men Are From Mars, Women Are From Venus*, notes that young children are totally vulnerable; they have no defense to the things we say and do; they receive everything. It seemed that Mark was also capable of judgment and decision as he reacted so intensely to that incident.

> What judgments and decisions have you made, about what you will say or do, based upon your childhood experiences?

When, as a child, have you been unable to speak? "What's the matter, cat got your tongue?" "What's wrong with you; speak up and answer me!" Where have you been embarrassed, laughed at, overpowered or ridiculed by those you trusted? How many times have you lost your voice and been dumb? What decisions did you make based on those situations that limit how you express yourself now?

In some families, the child's natural exuberant expression and joy of living can be controlled and limited. Do you remember hearing, "Children are to be seen and not heard?" How about these other little gems:

- "Don't think about it, just do it!"

- "Speak only when you're spoken to."

- "What would you know anyway; you're too young."

- "Do what I say, not what I do."

I recall being given the dunce's hat at school and made to wear it, sitting in a corner of the class room with my back to the other children. I felt ridiculous, unprotected and exposed as the others giggled at my glowing red ears. What decisions did I make that day that stuck me for years?

There may be times when you have bought into the lies that you can only be seen and not heard, must take action blindly and without awareness, can speak only in response and never speak out what you know, and more. Would this contribute to creating difficulty for you with speaking, performing and just, generally, being with people? How could you speak out as you, if you have never been recognized, acknowledged and appreciated for being you? How many people say to you, "I am so grateful that you have showed up in my life; thank you for being you." Any? Well, dear reader, Thank you for you.

The Deterrents

Do you know what soap tastes like? Yuk! Did your parents teach what is good to say, what is bad to say, what is right to say and what is wrong to say with the reward and punishment system? Except, they mostly forgot to reward you when you did it right for them and always remembered to punish you when you did it wrong for them. What are all the deterrents of you that were the hard love, the be cruel to be kind attitude the "It's for his own good." justifications and all of the "You'll thank me one day." lies you were told. Where are all the places that you tried to do it right for them and were always judged as wrong? Will you give up trying to be right for your parents, or anyone else, and consider being you, for you?

> How many times have you had your mouth washed out with soap for speaking the unspeakable?

> In how many lifetimes has your body been sliced by the belt, slashed with the cane, bruised with the boot, cut with the whip, smacked with the hand and beaten with the fist for what you've said? What will it take for you to be free from that?

Crowds

Many people begin to get nervous about speaking out, when there are four or more people in the group they are with. What number of people is it for you, before you become uncomfortable when speaking to groups—

more than one person, two people, three people, four people, ten people…?

In most groups there are often the speakers and the listeners, and the listeners generally outnumber the speakers. "Well," I hear you say "if everyone spoke at the same time then no one would hear anything." That's an interesting view. The question is, would you prefer to remain silent; a listener or be heard?

> What have you calculated the number of people it is safe to speak in front of?

The Spartacus warrior-slaves of old were renowned for their ability and skill in battle. They defeated armies much larger than their own numbers. In the last battle they fought, in Lucania, where they were outnumbered by Roman troops many times over, they fought down to the last few warriors before being overwhelmed and routed completely.

> What have you calculated is the number of people you can resist before being overwhelmed and destroyed?

How many people have you decided you can fend off with words before you will have to fight or run? And do you fight your own, personal battle with public speaking and speaking in groups?

Is listening quietly a way that you make you invisible and unnoticed so as not to become the focus of any possible assault?

How many times have you been shouted down, knocked down and trampled on while trying to speak of peace? Will you give it up please, step to one side and let those who choose it, go to war?

This may seem a little dramatic; over the top and may not even apply to you, but for some, I know it will. Maybe not the Spartacus example specifically, but other battles, other places and childhood experiences that you have forgotten but still affect you.

At the age of 57, I got free of a decision that I made at a young age. That decision and others built on top of it affected much more than just my speaking ability. With the foundational decision gone, the others had no support and tumbled. To be free of it is a gift beyond measure and has allowed a joyful peace to enter every part of my life. I am grateful.

Never give up. Every choice you make creates changes that allow more choice. There is no one choice that makes your public performance (or your life) perfect, but there is the ongoing adventure of what you choose.

Fight or Flight

Sympathetic Reactions

When you stand up to speak and experience "nerves," is it really *you* reacting or your body? If you will have that you are not your body, then it is probably your body. The body's instinctual survival response, when it perceives danger, is fight-or-flight.

> "The fight-or-flight response (also called the fight, flight, freeze or fawn response, hyperarousal, or the acute stress response) is a physiological reaction that occurs in response to a perceived harmful event, attack or threat to survival."—Wikipedia, from Walter Cannon 1932

When you place your body in front of an audience, is the body perceiving danger from the audience, or from *you* imagining that the audience is dangerous? When you flag something as dangerous, your body will disregard its own awareness in favor of yours; after all, you're supposed to know what you're doing, right?

A sympathetic nervous system

When you trigger flight-or-fight the body actions an extraordinary sequence of responses, beginning with a general discharge of the sympathetic nervous system, and undergoes rapid change. As the sympathetic nervous system goes to work, a variety of physiological systems are stimulated. Here's a concise listing:

- acceleration of heart and lung action
- paling or flushing, or alternating
- digestion slows down or stops
- general effect on the sphincters of the body
- blood vessels constrict in many parts of the body
- liberation of energy sources and dilation of blood vessels, for muscular action
- inhibition of tear and saliva production
- dilation of pupil and tunnel vision
- relaxation of bladder
- loss of hearing
- shaking

Do you recognize these as some of the effects that people who are experiencing difficulty with speaking suffer?

What I'd like you to get here is that these symptoms are the *body's sympathetic response to you!* So, it would make sense to look at what you are doing to create this, rather than trying to handle the body.

What are you doing?
When your body responds with fight-or-flight and you're not aware of what it's doing, you can believe that it's you; that it's you who is nervous or nauseous

or shaking, for example. Then, you become the effect of what your body is creating.

Bodies have their own awareness and share information with you. Your body lets you know when it's time to go to the bathroom, for example, and you can override that and not go. Your body can also alert you to danger.

Your viewpoint, thoughts, imagined fears, etc., can have a powerful effect on your body, and when *you* create an alert, *one that is not real*, then your body can't locate the danger and defers to you. It will respond as if the danger that you have imagined is real; your body prepares to fight-or-flight.

You, however, override the body because you don't fight or flight and begin using the resources that it's providing. You stay on-stage instead of running. Your body has no idea what you are doing; it's all ready to go but you stand rooted to the spot—you have to make your speech, right? Your brain won't function, vision becomes constricted, dry mouth, etc. As you do not react, your body pumps more adrenalin into the bloodstream…and you know the rest.

A situation can be created where you both become the effect of each other. Perhaps you have seen a body lost for words, rooted to the spot, frozen in the spotlight or struck dumb?

Many of the techniques offered to help you cope with these sorts of situations are about handling the symptoms of fight-or-flight and calming the body down. Deep-breathing, for example, thinking about something else, meditation, vigorous activity to use up adrenalin and others can work to assist the body to begin deactivating the sympathetic nervous system.

Treating symptoms though, is about handling what has already happened. What if you didn't have to go there in the first place?

The "un-nervous" nervous system
Where the sympathetic nervous system is responsible for stimulation, the parasympathetic nervous system handles "rest and digest" or "feed and breed" activities; it works to create calming, rest, conserving energy and rebuilding resources.

Here are some of its functions:

- increases digestion, intestinal motility, fuel storage
- strengthens resistance to infection
- facilitates rest and recuperation
- provides greater circulation to the skin and extremities
- boosts endorphins, the "feel good" hormones
- decreases heart rate
- reduces blood pressure and temperature

Can you see that this system is designed to create a different effect in the body? So, your body has one system that is more like the accelerator pedal in your car and another works more like the brake.

Choices
Your choices to raise alerts, imagined or real, will cause your body to respond accordingly, and will effect your

ability to function as a speaker. Both systems can be useful to you when you are aware of how they function and what turns them on.

The sympathetic nervous system can provide you with additional energy and resources with which to intensify your speaking, but too much of that will work against you. There can be a synergy with both where in the context of speaking, there is movement between these two complimentary systems, so that your body can rise to action and then fall to rest and then rise back to action, as required.

Good speaking includes a rise and fall of energy, volume, intensity, gestures and general activity. These nervous systems can assist you with that.

Being aware of how your body functions, and its willingness to assist you, will go a long way to creating you as a better speaker. You need to realize and acknowledge that the speeches you deliver are, in fact, created in a partnership between you and your body. Did you think it was just you, up there on stage?

Your body will contribute to your speaking if you consciously include it and are aware of what it can do. Fight-or-flight is just one of many capacities your body has; ignore it at your peril.

The Messenger

Don't Shoot Me!

When you have the attitude that you're "delivering" a speech, it can create particular dynamics that may put you at risk.

Messengers deliver messages, postmen deliver letters and couriers deliver parcels; and the obvious connection here is delivery. What is it? Delivery means to "hand over to another." When a speaker hands over their speech then, just like a messenger, they are simply passing it on, verbatim; word-for-word. A messenger is not the originator, but represents the originator and recites a predefined message to the recipient.

Who are you representing when you speak, why would it put you at risk and what can you do about it?

The Messenger

"Hey, don't shoot me, I'm just the messenger!" We are all familiar with the saying: Just because I am the one delivering bad news doesn't mean I created it.

Being a messenger can be risky because the reply to a delivered message can often be the messenger's severed head!

If you think that functioning as a messenger is a good idea, then be aware. The messenger is at risk because, the person who sent it is often the *least valuable member* of an organization. Kings do not send their most prized warriors to deliver messages; they send someone they can afford to lose. If a warrior is sent, they are accompanied by a large part of the army, with the size of the accompaniment in proportion to their high value. When the King arrives, the whole army is present. It is no wonder that you get off-stage as quickly as you can once you have delivered your speech. You may be running for your life!

You can see this type of handover speech in politics, where government representatives—ministers, senators, presidents—read speeches that have been written for them by someone else; speechwriters. These representatives deliver the message by reading off a sheet of paper. In some cases they may have rehearsed to make it seem more natural, and in recent years President Obama has become adept at working with a teleprompter (you may like to search YouTube to find several amusing videos of what happens when the President's teleprompter stops working).

> "…speechwriters became a permanent staple of presidential staffs when radio became the dominant national medium. Radio, television, cable television and the Internet have dramatically increased the frequency and reach of presidential pronouncements…"—Robert Schlesinger, author of *White House Ghosts*.

Messenger-type speeches are a part of modern day communications and some messengers are incredibly skillful at delivering them. Some are considered to be the greatest speeches of all time.

> "...a great political speech should speak to you and make you a part of its time and place. John Lindsay's second inaugural address as New York City's mayor does that. So does John F Kennedy's "Poetry and Power" speech, which sings, and Barbara Johnson's speech making the case for Richard Nixon's impeachment, which sears. But there is one speech which does all of these – sing, sear, speak and soar – sometimes simultaneously and, as a result, stands alone: President Abraham Lincoln's second inaugural address, delivered on the East Portico of the White House on March 4, 1865. It is my favorite political speech of all time."— Christian Nwachukwu, Jr. Senior speechwriter.

It would seem that *keeping your head on your shoulders* can be achieved successfully using remarkable talent and ability in the art of delivering speeches, and taking "messenger" to the highest levels.

Psychic Possibilities

Is It Really Yours?

When you are in a situation where a lot of other people are creating nerves, stresses or anxiety you may find yourself reacting without realizing where it's coming from. If you accept it as yours then it can create difficulty for you and your body. What if none of it was yours?

In the following story, about a speech competition, consider that not only were the competitors nervous, but anxious audience members (moms, dads and other supporters) also contributed to the charged atmosphere.

Despite actively participating in Toastmasters for about three years, I still was nervous, particularly before giving a speech. It wasn't until I attended an Access Consciousness workshop that I got clear on what was occurring for me. We may be far more psychic than we realize.

Beverly Brown, the class facilitator, described that many of the thoughts we have can come from someone else and that we have the ability to pick up other people's thoughts. She said that we may not always hear the words, sometimes just perceiving the energy of their thoughts or emotions.

You may recall saying something and your friend looks at you and replies, "I was just about to say that." or you were listening to someone talk and then completed the sentence for them without realizing you had spoken. My Dad will often pick up the phone and say, "Hello son." without me saying a word. Weird? So, if you are picking up other people's thoughts and thinking that they are yours, what effect is that having on you and your body? Interesting thought!

In 2004, having won my club's (Gold Coast Toastmasters) annual "International" speech competition, I was eligible to participate in the Gary Muller speech competition. This annual event is open to all speaking clubs in Gold Coast City, where I lived at the time.

On the night, I was drawn to speak last out of nine competitors. The audience was about 100 strong. As I sat through the other eight speeches and waited my turn I was aware of a lot of nerves in the room.

With each bout of nerves that I began to experience, I used a technique that I had learned at Beverly's class. In my head, I simply returned all of those nerves to-sender and found that my body and I calmed down each time. I repeated this whenever I felt nervous and when, finally, I was called to the stage I was relaxed and at ease in my body.

I narrowly missed the win that night but was delighted with second place. I realized that by being aware these were not all my nerves, I was able to function more from the parasympathetic and not be the effect of the sympathetic nervous system. The [1]fight-or-flight response was not triggered and my body and I both had a much easier and enjoyable time.

Explore the technique yourself. If you are feeling anxious say, "Everything that this is, I return it all to sender." Maybe you're more psychic than you realize.

---

1   Refer to the chapter, "Fight or Flight."

Stephen Outram

Amateurs & Professionals

Emotive, Technical or Holistic

There is an expectation that a professional will perform to or beyond certain measurable standards and there will be a level of consistency in what they do, which is above average or beyond the "norm." Spectators will pay to see professionals perform. Amateurs can be excused for their performances; they are expected to be below standard and are rarely paid. When a professional reaches a very high standard, for instance an elite athlete, they can command very large sums of money for appearing.

> "In 2001 and the early part of '02, Tiger [Woods] will make at least $10 million in appearance fees — compare that with the Tour single-season winnings record of $8.2 million he won in 2000."—USA Today

In 2005, Australia golfer Adam Bradley turned professional. Prior to that, while playing as an amateur in a Pro-Am competition, he had won a tournament but was unable to claim the cash prize; it was not allowed. It seems that a significant distinction around money is made between amateur and professional. Some might say that Adam deserved the money, but clearly, only the pros get paid.

Professional sports personalities, as amateur speakers, can be paid generously for their speeches. They have proved themselves professionals in the sports arena and their below-standard speaking performance is acceptable to promoters and audiences. An amateur, however, seldom receives payment for their effort and will often perform for no-fee, to gain experience or just for the love of it.

> Where have you been using amateur status as an excuse, limiting your income and speaking possibilities?

Amateur Speakers

The meaning of amateur is "a lover of any art or science, though not a professor [high-level teacher]." An amateur; a lover, will often speak from emotion and experience fear, nerves, embarrassment, panic, doubt, self-criticism and occasionally fleeting moments of elation.

Performing can be a drama with nerves to overcome, fears to suppress and an audience to face up to. The time on stage is largely about using learned lines and delivering the words rapid fire to limit their exposure. The finale is such a relief that they rarely hear the applause and rush off-stage recalling all the things they did wrong, the lines that were forgotten and everything they could have done better.

Amateur speakers often approach the stage apprehensively, in awe; their "approach" can be timid and defensive suggesting they consider the task dangerous or risky. In stark contrast, native hunters armed only with simple spears approach their prey with care. They are fully aware of the animal and are totally present in the moment; they can admire its beauty and respect its capacity to kill.

To the observer, it may appear that the hunters are in great danger and there is enormous risk. The hunters, however, by taking the animal into their care and having high-regard for it, may claim it as their prize.

To be aware and present in the moment is to have no vestment in the outcome and no distracting thoughts of the past or future.

An amateur prefers to observe and keep the audience at a safe distance. When you are unwilling to take the audience into your care, hold them in regard and have respect, you will not see their beauty and will only see the danger; you will not be aware of the possibilities and instead create limitation. When you are willing to be present and aware of the audience, then you will not create the distance that separates you from claiming them as your prize.

Do you expect to fail? Do you have an expectation, for example, that every time you speak in groups it will be a disaster? Do you ensure the disaster occurs so that you can say "See! I told you I was no good at this." and be right once again? When you create an expectation, such as, "I'm always so nervous when I speak," you begin to create it, look for it to occur and "Hey. Presto." there it is again. When you are being totally present in the moment you cannot have expectation.

What expectations have you made more real than you? What expectations do you have that you use to try and create a predictable future?

Professional Speakers

Where the amateur speaks from emotion, the professional can speak *with* emotion (or force, or softness…). The professional is more a technician, a scientist and is unlikely to fall victim of their own thoughts and feelings.

They know that a loss of control or an angry dramatic outburst can result in diminished performance and cost them prize money or incur a penalty.

> NBA player Metta World Peace is reported in Cheat Sheet, "…he suffered one of his biggest fines in January 2003, when he was suspended for three games without pay and fined $35,000 by the NBA for hurling a television monitor and smashing a camera to pieces."—Emily Coyle

A professional speaker, singer or athlete will have practiced for many hours to hone their skills. They know what they have to do and can sometimes exceed their own high standards of performance. Politics and some sports encourage performers to taunt their opposition, to put the other off their game. They know the tricks-of-the-trade and are willing to use them. Speakers may study human and crowd behavior to better influence their audiences. They work at being the best they can be. Do you?

When an amateur "turns" professional, they have turned from a right-brain to a more left-brain approach.

Science tells us that the left brain hemisphere functions from logic and the right from emotion.

> What or how far would you have to *turn* to speak as a professional?

Highly successful professionals cease being a student of the game and begin to teach the game; they become the professor. Professionals who "retire from the game" can be well-paid to speak or coach.

> "I'm worth $5,000 a lecture, and other speakers are worth $30,000 or more for two reasons: the lecture circuit and free market economics."— Scott Berkun, from *Confessions of a Public Speaker*.

Holistic Speakers

Holistic means "no boundaries, crossing all borders." To gain a greater sense of the word I refer you to J.C. Smuts, who in his book *Holism and Evolution* describes a process of "...unification of separate parts; from the Greek holos meaning 'whole.'" It seems to me that holistic will work to pull together or unify amateur and professional and that a person speaking holistically can apply any or all of the possible attributes, as and when they choose.

And that is what we're looking for here, choice. For you to have the choice to use anything that will work for you, be it raw emotion or technical expertise. And for you to be able to have that available to you *in the moment*, when it's required.

Sometimes you will need to stand back, create some distance and observe; and at other times you will be right up close, where you can smell the tiger's breath and hear his throaty gurgle. Sometimes you will require some right-brain softness and another time left-brain analytics, and yet another will demand a whole brain function.

Seek to be aware of everything that you can be, and choose.

Stephen Outram

Receiving Applause

An Audience's Gift

The majority of amateurs, after delivering a speech, put their heads down and move off-stage as quickly as possible; they flee. They have made little or no connection with the audience, have talked at the audience and are unwilling to receive the applause.

The professional seeks to create rapport, empathy and connection and will remain on stage to bathe in the applause. They bow, curtsy, blow kisses, smile, open their arms and soak it up like warm sunshine in winter; they allow the audience to appreciate the gift that they are. They are willing to receive. Are you?

Almost all learning or amateur speakers cannot receive applause, because they are unwilling to acknowledge their own greatness; that their speech was worthy or valuable to someone. It would seem that, in the first place, the speech was not valued or applauded by them.

That which you will not receive can become a barrier to you having it from anyone or anything else.

This is an important concept and you may like to review it several times. Looking at it from another direction, for example, someone I know is adorable and everyone says so. Why? Because this friend is *being* adorable; she creates that. If she was not being adorable we could not adore her; she is willing to be adored and receive adoration from others. If she did not acknowledge and value her own adorableness, then no one else would be able to either.

Let's explore "receiving" and see how it applies in public speaking.

Receiving

I was first introduced to the concept of receiving during a seminar given by Gary Douglas. He described that receiving is a capacity we have. It's not about "getting" something, which is a one-way flow; it is a gifting and receiving all at the same time.

When someone gives you a gift, what they really desire is that you simply receive it from them. If I gave you a large sum of money, no strings attached, and you said, "Gosh! I can't take that. It's too much." then you are refusing or not receiving my gift; you have judged the money inappropriate. In so doing, you have begun erecting a barrier; the limitation of you having more money in your life. In addition, as the giver of inappropriate gifts, you have rejected me.

I was having coffee with a friend in a street-side boutique when I noticed, across the road, an old man had fallen down. I left my friend and ran over to him to see if I could assist.

He had been walking slowly along with the aid of a walking frame and the wheel had slipped off the footpath into a garden bed; he had toppled to land firmly on the concrete footpath. Ouch!

I knelt down, put my hand on his shoulder and asked if he was hurt, and may I assist him. The old man pushed my hand away and replied that he could handle it. I stood up and got his walking frame straightened up and put it back on the footpath near him. He gritted his teeth, rolled over and slowly, painfully pulled himself back up to standing. He complained to me about footpaths, seized his frame and moved away. What was it that he did not receive; my help or something else?

What he refused to receive was my caring; the gift that I cared enough to run across the road, to comfort his battered body and be with him while he was vulnerable. I didn't judge him; that he was a silly old fool for falling; I was simply there being me.

When I returned to my friend, she put her hand on my arm and smiled at me; an acknowledgment and it was the gift that the old man had been unable to provide. The old man could not receive caring, but he could receive that he was a silly old fool. If I had told him he was stupid for falling over, he probably would have accepted that! Oh well.

Gifting and receiving is an energetic connection; a flow that contributes to both.

Applause

Applause is a gift; it's the audience flowing energy at you in appreciation of your talk; your performance and of you. It is a great part of the communion you seek to have with the audience, and they with you. When you are willing to receive their gift, they can receive more of the gift of you. Then you create a gifting and receiving in simultaneity, which is expansive and glorious for all present.

Build the Muscle
Here are several things you may like to play with, which can provide you with a greater awareness of receiving. Beyond these, seek to be aware of when someone or something—a tree gifting shade on a hot day— is gifting to you, and simply receive it without judgment.

The Mirror
Create some time where you can be alone in your home, and in a comfortable place setup a large mirror where you can see yourself. Sit and look you right in the eye. Do this for an hour and be aware of all of the thoughts running through your head. Receive you by acknowledging the judgments that you have of yourself, and your body. Allow them to simply be there, you don't have to do anything with them. Be with them, receive them and allow them to dissipate.

Applaud You
Again, create some space where you can be home alone. Give a talk; a speech to your reflection in the mirror. When you are done applaud you; applaud for at least 10 minutes until your arms are weary and your hands tingle. Allow yourself to receive that applause and gift back to you.

Speeches
If you are a member of a speaking club, then rather than moving away from the lectern immediately you have finished your speech, stay a while and acknowledge your audience and their applause. Put a note in big letters at the end of your written speech, "Stay and receive the applause!" to remind you.

In Addition…
A high school teacher provided this personal story.

"A group of Year 10 boys were hanging-out on both sides of a walkway at school, and applauding loudly as staff and students walked through their group. Another teacher told me that she felt intimidated by them.

I chose to stand-in with them and asked individual boys to walk, taking turns, through the group to receive the applause. Each of them did and I went last; we chose to receive the applause.

I realized later, that we were all willing to receive, have fun and turned the activity into a game. What was the other teacher creating?

Characters of You

Who Are You Being?

We all have characters that are dusted off and presented in different situations; the many characters of you. You probably have already created a character to represent you when you are speaking, but who are you?

Two masks were worn by actors in ancient Greece around 500 - 300 BC. The traditional Comedy Tragedy masks are used now as a universal symbol for drama, and interestingly, represent the two effects of wine: joyous celebrations and a dark, grief-filled harvest. Professor Oliver Taplin of Magdalen College, Oxford; shares his insight into the masks.

Taplin notes that "Putting on the mask gave you some kind of licence, and also perhaps some kind of immunity." He also suggests that "...the mask was fundamentally the sign of the act of impersonation. By putting on the mask the actor declared that he was not just narrating the story but was doing the story."

> What story are you doing that is the impersonation of you?

While discussing a production of the play *Tantalus*, Taplin describes the two actors who used their masks most effectively, "...both stripped naked and took off their masks in a declaration of direct intimacy. The clear symbolism of this was that reality hides behind the mask, that the mask and costume "veil" the true self."

Do you veil your true self by acting out the many personas—all the masks—of you? At any one time you may be, for example, a daughter, a sister, an aunt, a mother and a wife. You switch from one role to the other without thinking about it; automatically and unconsciously.

People can be so skilled in these transformations that a mother can bend down to comfort her child and then rise to kiss her husband as a wife. In those few seconds, the child and husband perceive the character she was playing very differently? So who are you, really? Who is behind the masks?

In a small group like a family or at work, you can switch and change your masks so quickly that no one really notices. However, who do you act when in front of a larger group? Which character will you choose when in front of strangers? It can be confusing, because you don't know who to be for so many different people; most of whom you have never met before. In those situations, where you are more exposed, do you begin to get nervous, or do you have a speaking-in-groups character; one that you don't use very often and is a bit rusty?

> How many masks do you use to present the many characters of you?

The following two short stories describe three people creating different results with the speeches they make. After you have read the stories, consider which person has a speaking character ready?

The Wedding Speech

At my sister's wedding, during the speeches her new husband Ken was called-on to say a few words. It turned out to be a very few words as Ken had no experience in public speaking and was suddenly the focus of a group of about 80 people. He didn't know who to be for so many and, literally, ran out of words. His new wife stood up, put her arms around him and finished the speech. Several people commented to me later how easily and naturally she had spoken and that she had really connected with them. I realise now that she had spoken just like she normally does, as Karen, and we all knew her.

The Sports Speech

In another situation, a friend of mine who I used to play squash with got up to receive a sporting award. Bradley gave an amazing acceptance speech and it was like, "Wow! I didn't know you could speak like that. I hardly recognized you up there." As an active member of a community organization called Apex, Bradley was required to speak in their meetings; and he had his speaking-in-groups character well rehearsed.

Let's take a moment to review each of the three people in the stories:

1. From the moment Ken stood up and began talking, he got smaller and smaller and became lost for words. He had probably not spoken to a group larger than his family before and had no tools, no skills and no character to act. To survive the razor sharp focus of 80 pairs of eyes, it seemed that he had

disappeared and left his body there on the stage.

2. Karen did not judge her husband, as many of the guests did, when he began to falter. She stood to care for him and nurtured Ken in her arms. With this action she also took the audience into her care. She did not push him to one side to take over, but included him in their talk. She spoke as Karen, there was no mask and she knew who she was.

3. When Bradley spoke in acceptance on his award, it was a surprise.,"Who is that?" "Where did our friend go?" Who was this well spoken, charismatic and funny personality up there on the stage? Brad had written a speech and rehearsed it; he had his character well prepared.

None of these performances are wrong or bad. I'd like you to be aware what each creates: Ken was unable to function, Karen handled the moment with a great deal of ease, and Brad was able to function, though probably within the scope of his rehearsed speech.

How much energy does it take to maintain a wardrobe of many characters; functioning in a constant state of dress and undress; makeup-on, makeup-off; recite these old lines, learn some new lines; lights, action, camera and cut; new scene? Phew!

Being You
Who are you? Without all of the characters, masks and personas, what would you be like? And how much easier could it be for you to just be you; no acting required?

Let me ask you two complex questions and then consider how you feel; be aware of what you're perceiving.

> Are you substituting you by acting out various predefined roles; all the characters, the categories, the descriptions and the definitions of you that have you masquerading as the not-you?

> What will it take for you to show up as you where you wouldn't have to defend, protect or conceal anymore; and that creating the disguises of you would no longer be necessary?

What could be different if your audience were presented with all of you, the real you and would not be cheated by the lack of you? You would not have to get nervous about being exposed as a fraud or being caught-out; that is…being caught *out of character.*

Would it be easier to simply be you? And from that, choose what was required in each moment. It may be that an act will create the effect you desire, or a written speech is necessary, or even that being lost for words will get you out of doing something you don't want to do. The point is to have all of this, and more, available as a conscious choice and to cease functioning on autopilot.

One of my early speaking jobs was to provide one hour of training for an organization. I agreed and chose to present a free-form class. There is little form or structure in this type of class and I was seeking to generate questions from the audience and to work directly with their input.

I was quite nervous as I had no idea what might be asked and where it would go. I asked myself some simple questions, such as, "What is really going on here?" I realized that I wasn't willing to be judged, to fail and I doubted my own ability to be me and work in the moment with anything that came up. I also asked, "Okay. What is the worst that I can create?" The worst was that I might have to say to someone, "Sorry, I don't have an answer for you." I looked at other possible scenarios and after a while said to myself. "What would be different here if I did this just for fun and to see what shows up?" And that's what I went with.

It was great and I was able to speak as me, create connection, empower people and we had a lot of fun. I noticed that some people engaged with me and others did not; a few people day dreamed and one left the room to make phone calls. The ones that asked questions and contributed to creating the event received a lot themselves and provided much for the others. How does it get any better than that?

As a speaker, you will be judged and you have to be willing for that and to not buy into other people's judgments of you. The larger the audience the greater the judgment. Your capacity to be okay with that and let them have their judgments, will go a long way to you creating greater ease with public speaking. The masks may seem a good idea, but really, they are thin disguise.

Be willing to *not* have all the answers. There will be someone in the audience who knows more than you. Consider that you have an amazing and diverse resource, right there in front of you. Use it! When you get something you can't handle, ask you audience for help; include them and your events will be all the richer for it.

Indulge yourself in the worst case scenario. Look at it objectively and you will find that, often, it's a lot less of a drama than what you're imagining it to be.

Have fun! Be willing to be the only person in the room enjoying a good time. Do you recall the 1980s laughing bag I mentioned in another chapter? Well, having a good time can be highly contagious as well.

In fact, you having fun as you will be irresistible!

Stephen Outram

Heights Unimagined

Inclusive, Expanding Contribution

At the Winter Olympics in Torino, Italy 2006, Russians Navka and Kostomarov skated in the Free Dance competition. They began their programme and danced with superb skill and expression. As the music and the dance changed tempo, the audience saw an opportunity to participate and began to clap in time to the new rhythm. The audience transformed from passive observers to active ingredients in a delicious mix of music, dance and magic all being blended together by four razor sharp blades flashing across the ice.

The skaters lit-up, acknowledged their new partners and in so doing invited the audience to participate even more. This communion between performers and audience expanded, creating more possibilities and the skaters chose to be greater, grander and even more magnificent. The audience too, saw that there was more possible than they had imagined and rose and cheered, and then roared their applause as Navka and Kostomarov completed their final element … for a brief moment standing statuesque atop the glistening ice.

Everyone had completely forgotten the Winter Olympics, the competition, their lives and this reality in those exquisite moments of magic and possibility. They were totally present, in the moment and intimately connected.

This was a wonderful example of inclusive, expanding contribution that invites both audience and performers to create more than is possible apart.

In that Free Dance event there were the skaters and the audience; similarly in public speaking there is a speaker and the audience; you and those listening…what will you invite your audience to?

When performers include their audience and acknowledge them as co-creators, their contribution can lift the performance to heights unimagined. Surely, that is a target worth aiming for.

Navka and Kostomarov, and their audience, chose gold in 2006. What else is possible for you?

See over…

About The Author

Biography

Stephen Outram has a background of some 18 years in architecture, and since 1997 has worked as a graphic artist, website developer and Internet consultant. More recently he has written several books, spoken and presented seminars on a number of topics.

Educated in Queensland, Australia, Stephen studied at Brisbane's University of Technology in the 1970s. He returned to study in 1995 at Dundee University, Scotland, achieving a Master of Science degree in Computing.

Stephen was an active member of Toastmasters where he became President of Gold Coast Toastmasters Club, representing the club in speaking competitions and official events.

His family emigrated to Australia, from the United Kingdom in 1965, originally landing in Freemantle, Western Australia and spending 5 years in the northerly town of Port Hedland. In 1970 the family drove across the country from west to east and settled in Queensland's Gold Coast, where his parents and sister still reside.

Stephen enjoys a diverse and wide range of projects including work, writing, music and song writing, boats and some sport. He is active with Surfrider Foundation Australia and is interested in sustainable and flourishing coastlines and waterways, free of plastics and pollution.

For more information, visit the website:

stephenoutram.com

Stephen Outram

Toastmasters

Speaking & Leadership Skills

I will add a note here about Toastmasters International.

Toastmasters have developed and refined an outstanding educational program, which functions within a "club" model, and can assist you to gain skill and practical experience in a supportive environment.

Individual clubs function within a hierarchy of National and International management, which provides members with more and more responsible roles, where they can progress "up the ladder" if they desire that. It is club level that I will discuss briefly here.

I joined Toastmasters to learn, improve my practical speaking, gain experience and hopefully quell my nervousness during public appearances. I progressed through the various offered roles to become President of Gold Coast Toastmaster Club and went on to represent the club in many speaking competitions and other events.

There are many fine people who are members of Toastmasters and it is easy to make friends and enjoy the social aspect of club life, as well as speaking.

I certainly recommend this organization to people who are seeking to improve their speaking. It is very good and provides a great deal at a relatively low cost.

My opinion is that Toastmasters has some limitations, in the sense that the program works well within a club environment. If you desire to become a professional speaker then at some point you may require additional training and engagement beyond the comfort of club.

In Toastmasters I gained tools and experience that helped me to manage my fears, but those fears did not go away or become less intense. That was achieved by a relentless search on my part, to get to the core of my difficulties. It has *not* been a habit of mine to treat symptoms, but to seek greater awareness and make different choices.

I encourage you to review Toastmasters; visit clubs in your area as a guest and select one that appeals to you. And be aware that a headache tablet can only mask the pain and may not get to the source of your discomfort.

I am grateful for Toastmasters and the many people I met and worked with while I was active there.

Toastmasters is available in most countries of the world and you can find more information at their website.

www.toastmasters.org

Related Books

Advanced Speaking Concepts

Written for people who are seeking to create something greater and something different with public speaking, it will also benefit people who are beginning; the new generation of speakers.

This book contains ideas and concepts that can assist you in going beyond all of the old, worn public speaking techniques that everyone else uses to be competent, average and safe.

- Exposed! The myth that public speaking is the No.1 fear.
- The weird and *hidden issues* that are holding you back.
- Nerves! Why you need them to perform better.
- Applause. A beginning, not the end.
- Manipulation! Using it to advantage.

What if your journey with public speaking was really an adventure unfolding before you with each new choice you make?

More information at stephenoutram.com

www.ingramcontent.com/pod-product-compliance
Lightning Source LLC
Chambersburg PA
CBHW020008050426
42450CB00005B/375